Praise for *Leading T*

"In *Leading Through Free Fall*, Brianna Sylver goes beyond process to confront the real barrier to innovation: human resistance to change. With clarity and candor, she helps leaders navigate the emotional white-water rapids that no framework can fix. This is a vital handbook for executives who need their teams to move faster, adapt smarter, then act with curiosity, confidence, and courage."

LARRY KEELEY, innovation scientist, Keeley Innovations; co-founder, Doblin; adjunct professor, Institute of Design, Illinois Tech; author, *Ten Types of Innovation*

"Great ideas often get stalled—not because they're weak, but because they're surrounded by too much ambiguity and uncertainty. Brianna Sylver is that rare, wise guide who knows how to lead teams through change with clarity and heart. This book should be read by anyone managing innovation under pressure."

PATRICK WHITNEY, Dean Emeritus, Institute of Design, Illinois Tech; Distinguished Senior Fellow, Brown University School of Public Health

"Practical, grounded, and human, Brianna Sylver shows how instinct and intuition shape leadership that thrives in the uncertainty of innovation."

ROB VOLPE, founder and CEO, Ignite 360; empathy activist; author, *Tell Me More About That*

"In the face of rapid change and internal resistance, *Leading Through Free Fall* provides a powerful framework for unlocking progress. Brianna Sylver shows you how to reframe roadblocks, align teams, and lead transformation efforts that stick—by focusing on the human dynamics at the core of innovation."

VIJAY KUMAR, author, *101 Design Methods*

"This book fills a significant gap in practice—how do innovation leaders prepare the organization and set the conditions for success? The advice is clear, grounded, and practical. Innovation leaders of all levels will benefit from it. It's the total package."

KIM ERWIN, Director, Equitable Healthcare Lab, Institute of Design, Illinois Tech; author, *Communicating the New*

"In a culture that glorifies visionary leaders, Brianna Sylver brings something rarer: clarity, candor, and a deeply human approach. Her framework doesn't just guide innovation—it steadies leaders through the stunning discomfort of innovation, making the journey more intentional, strategic, and real."

PRISCILLA MCKINNEY, CEO, Little Bird Marketing; author, *Collaboration Is the New Competition*

"Brianna Sylver's refreshing honesty is a welcome shift from similar leadership books; it forced me to stop several times and reflect on my own actions and plans as an innovation leader. It's a must-read for anyone driving innovation in the real world—authentic, personal, engaging, and thoughtful."

ANIJO MATHEW, Dean, Institute of Design, Illinois Tech

"Brianna Sylver is the leader we need speaking on innovation in business at this pivotal moment. Her deep experience shines through every page of *Leading Through Free Fall*, offering a clear, grounded path for bringing bold ideas to life—while also keeping the process creative and calm."

HEATHER DOMINICK, author, *Different*

"Every innovation leader faces turbulence. *Leading Through Free Fall* gives you the mindset, tools, and courage to lead anyway."

WILL LEACH, CEO, Mindstate Group; author, Marketing to Mindstates

Leading
Through
Free Fall

How Innovators Turn Turbulence into Trust

Leading Through Free Fall

BRIANNA SYLVER

●● PAGE TWO

Cataloguing in publication information is available from Library and Archives Canada.
ISBN 978-1-77458-595-5 (paperback)
ISBN 978-1-77458-596-2 (ebook)

Page Two
pagetwo.com

Page Two™ is a trademark owned by Page Two Strategies Inc., and is used under license by authorized licensees

Cover design by Taysia Louie
Interior design and illustrations by Fiona Lee

sylverconsulting.com

To God—the true source of all light and love.

May this work serve as a reflection of

Your purpose, reminding us to be the salt of

the earth and the light of the world, as

You have called us to be (Matthew 5:13–16).

In Your strength and for Your glory,

this book is dedicated.

Contents

On the Runway *1*

PART ONE **SUITING UP**

▸ Part One Introduction *13*

1 Scope with Your Eyes Open *15*

2 Meet Your Stakeholders
Where They Are *25*

3 Slay Energy Vampires *37*

4 Define Project Success *47*

5 Clarify Innovation Ambition *59*

6 Use Past Experiences to
Direct the Future *71*

7 Define Your Core Leadership Values *85*

PART TWO **FREE FALL**

▸ Part Two Introduction *101*

8 Tame the Skeptics *103*

9 Own Your Strengths *115*

10   Watch Your Frog *129*

11   Evolve in Real Time *143*

12   Weather the Blamestorm *153*

13   Manage Timeline Change Requests *167*

14   Pause When Leadership Shifts Occur *181*

PART THREE   **SAFE LANDING**

▸   Part Three Introduction *195*

15   Empower Implementation Partners *197*

16   Create and Sustain
     Implementation Momentum *209*

17   Let Go *221*

     Earn Your Wings *231*

     Acknowledgments *235*

     Notes *239*

On the Runway

WHEN I BEGAN this book journey, I was hopeful, excited, and full of joy and optimism. The creativity was flowing, and I felt high on it. Things were clicking into place. All was smooth sailing, forward momentum, and optimistic anticipation.

Until May.

With most of an initial manuscript written and the end in sight, the original publisher of this book went bankrupt. I went from having a contract—a path forward that was certain—to living in the space of ambiguity: Will this book ever come to be?

I felt utterly defeated. Maybe this was the universe's way of saying, "You're not supposed to write this book, Brianna. Hang it up and move on." I spiraled for a week, wallowing in my own self-pity. And then I got tired of myself and decided it was time to pull up my big-girl pants and recommit to the mission of making sure this book and its message went out into the world.

Then, a week later, just as my energy was rebounding from the blow of the loss of the publisher, one of my clients tried to commit suicide. Thankfully, by the grace of God, he survived. But I was now left with a very "hot" and charged project, midstream, without a project owner. The organization itself was in free fall and lots of internal separation tactics left me standing on a limb by myself, questioning: *Why am I committed to this project? Am I meant to stay the course or flee?* I engaged in some major dialogues with God on that one, as my reputation was under attack and the stress was taking a major toll on my own health and wellness. Yet, the message I received was clear: I was meant to stay the course and continue to lean in, despite the chaos and turmoil around me.

Then some intense team dynamics reared their head within my own organization, Sylver Consulting. Some of our internal systems had reached their capacity limits. While those systems had served us well in the past, it was clear that they wouldn't support us in the future. I'd love to tell you that everyone jumped onboard for the system change graciously and effortlessly. But that's not what happened. Some figurative kicking and screaming occurred—both from myself, as the leader, and from my team members. It took a couple of months to weather that storm.

And then a client didn't love the results of a project we were working on. The campaign they were about to launch wasn't resonating with the level of differentiation that they wanted to see. Instead of using that knowledge as the impetus for reflection and pivot, they attacked the research methodology, tried to undermine and sabotage the work, and outright asked us to delete data points from the data set—all to save face in front of their senior leaders and avoid rework. It was a mess, fraught with a series of moral and ethical tensions that had to be managed with great care and sensitivity.

And this is just a snapshot, a subset of the "thens" that were happening at this very challenging time. For months, I felt like I was living under a dark cloud—waiting, hoping, praying for a little bit of light to shine through.

The strange blessing of that time was that *so much* was going haywire and nearly all of it was out of my control. My typical MO—roll up my sleeves, jump in, get to fixing—wasn't going to work. For so many of these situations, there was no fix. While I could control the way in which I responded to the mayhem, I had so little influence over what was creating it.

I don't wish on anyone the abundance of challenges that were dominating my life at that moment. It was intense! Yet, the sheer volume of these challenges—happening all at once—underscored the importance and value of this book for me.

Innovation roadblocks and challenges are going to happen. It's not *if* you'll face them. It's *when*. And humans are at the core of most of the tension, turmoil, and turbulence that you'll experience. Humans with real fears, anxieties, and resistance. Humans who can't be removed from the process. Or ignored. Or avoided, in hopes they'll disappear.

The Messy Humanness of Innovation

While we innovation leaders *love* and know how to spearhead innovation processes, we don't always love or know what to do with the humans in that process.

Yes, we can explain the Double Diamond approach to innovation. We can talk about innovation theory until we're blue in the face. But we can't create a predictable process around the human experience of innovation.

So, what do we do instead? We tend to avoid the human issues that pop up in our innovation work. With our fingers crossed and a quick, desperate prayer, we attempt to plow through the tension and discomfort that emerges in our work. If we don't acknowledge it, it'll disappear, right?

Sadly, the answer is no. Avoidance and denial only get you so far. In fact, they often make matters worse. While you might eventually arrive at the hoped-for outcome, the journey will be fraught with unnecessary struggle, anxiety, and frustration. The results will be watered down. Your team will be exhausted. You'll want to quit.

If you've been in the role of innovation leader for any amount of time, you've likely faced some of the challenges I've described. You've likely felt exhausted, defeated, and confused a number of times. You've likely questioned the crazies around you—*What is wrong with these people?!* And you've also likely questioned yourself—*Why is this happening to me? Am I not a good leader? Am I doing something wrong?*

Let me assure you, the only thing you're doing wrong is buying into the lie that the innovation process *should be* smooth, that a successful innovation process is one without hiccups. The idea that the innovation process can be tamed or controlled is an absolute myth. You might have smooth-sailing moments, moments when you're making all the right moves in all the right places, when your team is aligned and stakeholders are excited, when all you can see is bright-blue skies all around. But these moments are rare... and fleeting.

At the end of the day, you're dealing with the crazy combination of humans in the midst of change. And *no one* seamlessly embraces change, even innovation changemakers like us. Humans, as a species, are hardwired to resist change, even when we know it is imminent and ultimately good for us.

Your role as an innovation leader is to guide humans through the innovation process and tame the anxieties and fears that will inevitably pop up through that journey. You're not just leading the creation of an idea, process, or product. You're leading humans—through or toward something new.

Your role as an innovation leader is to guide humans through the innovation process and tame the anxieties that will inevitably pop up through that journey.

A New Measure of Success

Change, for most humans, is difficult. It can cause uncertainty and discomfort. People can feel nervous or threatened and express those feelings through unhelpful actions, such as procrastination, passive-aggression, or refusal to engage with new processes or ideas.

I've written this book to acknowledge that you will be met with resistance in your role as an innovation leader. I hope to prepare you for how to respond to that resistance with love and compassion. I want to arm you with a host of tools and resources that will help you and your stakeholders to embrace each roadblock and challenge as the gift it is intended to be.

Hold up... did I just refer to roadblocks and challenges as *gifts*? Indeed, I did!

Each innovation roadblock or challenge is a gift that you get to unwrap and examine with intention. It's an opportunity for you, as the innovation leader, to ask yourself: *What lesson(s) am I meant to be learning here? Why is this happening* for *me?* (Notice that I did not say *to* me.)

When we shine light on the human dynamics underlying a roadblock or challenge, we instantly defang it. Only then can we deal with the fears and anxieties holding the project back as problems to be solved—collectively, as a group. Yet, when we choose not to see (or more often *pretend* not to see) the unhelpful dynamics at play in projects, we give these things more power and undermine our ability to create the desired outcomes of our work.

I'm going to show you, throughout this book, how to unwrap and examine each roadblock and challenge for the lessons you—and your organization and your key stakeholders—are meant to learn.

But here's the thing: I'm inviting you into a choice point for yourself. You, as a leader of innovation, will need to consciously and continually challenge yourself to be more vulnerable and introspective. It will feel uncomfortable. You will wonder, *Will this really work?* You're going to get cold feet.

From experience, I can share that when you bravely and courageously unpack each challenge given to you, the rewards are tenfold—more buy-in for your work, more alignment moving forward, and greater impact overall. You'll see this in action in the stories throughout this book. But it's one thing to tell you what this might look like. It's another thing entirely for you to put yourself out there and try it. I nudge you to do just that. Be bold and courageous. Lead a discussion or workshop, as I suggest in this book, and then track the outcomes. See for yourself.

Champion of Change

As an innovation leader, you've assumed the calling of a changemaker. This means more than pushing a change through; you're also responsible for other people's experience through the innovation process. You're a coach and it is your job to meet people where they are and move them to a better future state, one full of promise and light.

To support you in this charge, innovator, I want you to visualize yourself as a Care Bear with love shining from your belly, inviting all stakeholders to the circle of change, no matter their starting point. Why a Care Bear? (I know, it sounds cheesy.) Because it works.

When I visualize myself as a Care Bear, I'm empowered to show up as the best version of myself. I shine loving light and optimistic energy, resulting in a more positive energetic experience for the teams I'm supporting. It leads me to ask more productive questions: *Why are people resistant at this moment? Why aren't they with me? Am I meant to change and adapt? Do I need to pause and allow people to bring their feelings to the table?*

When you embody this Care Bear energy, you start approaching tension differently. This isn't about you; it's about helping those you're working with to navigate discomfort with resilience—rather than following automatic responses, like avoiding, digging their heels in, and playing the blame game.

And this book is about helping you to be that leader of light. The tools it gives you help surface the tensions that threaten to take your innovation work off course. Each tool is designed to help you hash out those tensions and to use them to create deeper partnerships and openness to change among your stakeholder teams.

Your Innovation Playbook

For over twenty years, I've been supporting teams through innovation, operating at the intersection of user experience, market research, and strategy. I work with organizations seeking clarity on what next steps to take to yield the growth and outcomes that they desire. They often feel uneasy about where they are. They know that change isn't optional; it's imminent. Yet, they also don't know what it looks like to change. They might have a sense of where they want to be or, more appropriately, what will be true when they've "arrived" (more growth, more connection with their customers, more market share in their industry, etc.). However, the pathway to get to that desired outcome is foggy to opaque.

This is where I thrive: guiding teams in understanding the obstacles standing in the way of their growth goals, defining the pathway of change, and aligning stakeholders around those new visions for growth. When clients work with my organization, Sylver Consulting, they gain confidence and clarity on what their next steps should be and can successfully advocate and lead their organization in that defined pathway of change.

This isn't a book about innovation process. I don't think our industry needs another innovation *process* book. This is a playbook, filled with tools that have helped me acknowledge, honor, and embrace the human challenges within the process of facilitating innovation. It's a guide for how to lean into and navigate the turbulent winds inherent in the innovation process. It's a resource that shows you how to emerge with grit, grace, and joy, in spite of or despite the turbulent winds that will occur and threaten to take you off course and water down, if not full-on trample, your impact.

In the first part of this book, "Suiting Up," we'll talk about different ways to set yourself up for success. These are markers you can come back to throughout your projects—when you're feeling ungrounded, when the project starts to go off the rails, when your team members get sidetracked, and so on. In the second part, "Free Fall," we'll talk through many of the challenges that arise in the middle of an innovation journey. We'll discuss ways you can face these obstacles head-on instead of sticking your head in the sand or ignoring the elephant in the room. In the final part, "Safe Landing," we'll address the transition into implementation and how to ensure that others pick up the reins and finish strong.

This book isn't a program to be followed through step-by-step. Its chapters are focused on different experiences that can arise during the innovation process. Each chapter is self-contained, so you can return to whichever one you need, time and again, when you're struggling to embrace and honor the messy humanness that runs as an undercurrent beneath every innovation initiative. In each chapter, I'll share real stories of each innovation roadblock in action. I'll help you understand the human issues that were happening beneath the surface of that specific challenge and how my team and I moved through that situation, ultimately reaching the other side with greater clarity and cohesion. This moving through often involves specific activities or workshops, but sometimes these are simply intentional discussions that bring the underlying human issues impacting the project to the surface. Regardless of the activity, workshop, or discussion used, the outcome always involves a shift in perspective, mindset shifts that can bolster your resilience and lead you through the turbulence from a confident, empowered place.

You might use the tools exactly as I've specified. But I also invite you to tweak them, change them, and make them your own. These exercises aren't meant to be templates. Rather, they're meant to help you consider a different way through, one that acknowledges and engages the humanness of the challenges you're facing and encourages you to bring those challenges into the light instead of allowing them to insidiously influence and impact actions from the backstage.

I also want to underscore that you do not need to commit to using *all* of these tools on every single project. Some are going to be relevant to you and others not, based on your project, your role, and the openness of your stakeholder teams.

My hope, however, is that after reading this book, you will commit to using at least one of the tools in an ongoing or upcoming project (just to get you started). And please, track your outcomes when you do. You'll begin to see challenges differently: not as unnecessary distractions but as opportunities to arrive at better outcomes. You'll be empowered to lead with more grounded energy and clear direction. And you'll rise to your purpose and calling of being a catalyst of change, not only for the organizations you work with, but for the individuals that you get to walk alongside. And for yourself, too.

PART ONE

Suiting Up

"Change is inevitable.
Growth is optional."

JOHN C. MAXWELL

EVERYBODY WANTS TRANSFORMATION, but no one *actually* wants to do the work of change. Because change is difficult. And uncomfortable. And it gives rise to all sorts of unpleasant feelings like insecurity, incompetency, anxiety, and uncertainty.

While you can't realistically prepare or plan for each turbulent wind that you'll experience in your innovation work, you can intentionally and consciously *set the stage for success*.

This is like getting ready to skydive. You need a jump plan. You wouldn't jump without putting your jumpsuit and harness on. You wouldn't jump without clearly mapping out your jump spot.

So why would you jump without doing the prep work in your innovation initiative?

Your responsibility as a leader of innovation is to suit up, to guide the definition of the drop zone, and to mark the jump spot. Helping you to do exactly that is the intent of this first section of the book.

In the coming pages, you'll learn how to work with your stakeholders to

- clearly state the problem that your innovation work is tackling;

- uncover both the obvious and hidden assumptions that your stakeholders have about the project or solution;

- spot and address project risks early, before they become major issues;

- define what success looks and feels like for your project, in terms of both results and experience.

By aligning fully with your stakeholders up front—on both your drop zone and your jump spot—you ready yourself to maintain momentum, no matter the obstacles ahead. You also increase the likelihood that the innovations emerging from your work get implemented within the org.

So, let's gear up and get ready! Developing core practices to *suit up for success* will strengthen the resilience of you and your team and increase your overall effectiveness at creating impactful and meaningful innovation.

1

Scope with
Your Eyes Open

HAVE YOU EXPERIENCED those projects where you find yourself or others asking *halfway through*, "What are we even trying to learn?" or "Why does this even matter?" This untethered feeling is super uncomfortable and anxiety-riddled.

The good news is that it's also completely avoidable. You can sidestep this fate if you put in the right work up front and approach your scoping and kickoff calls with curiosity and a healthy dose of skepticism.

Let's unpack that a bit ...

"Actionable insight" is the catchphrase that makes its way into every research or innovation brief and kickoff call. It's the Holy Grail that so many strive for, and yet, many often miss this mark. That's because most people think "actionable insight" is captured in project deliverables—the research, the solution, or the change itself. But this understanding is incomplete. "Actionable insight" can occur only if you, as the innovator, carefully curate the project's full engagement journey... and the first steps in that journey are scoping and kickoff.

At this stage of the "actionable insights" journey, you want to ask the challenging questions: *Why are you doing this? What's the broader business goal? What are the expectations and hopes that you have for this initiative?*

You pose the above questions with the intent to more clearly frame your initiative. What's the outcome your stakeholders are looking for? And *why* are they seeking that outcome? How will they use the output of your project as the input for other projects or business decisions?

Friends, this is a meeting that you need to be on point for. You cannot let someone else lead this meeting. And you need to dig deep in your questioning in the conversation. Do not accept anything at face value, as doing so allows for your stakeholder's blind spots to persist during the scoping process. If those blind spots turn out to be potholes of misunderstanding and erroneous assumptions, that's when you'll find yourself in the middle of the project asking those dreaded questions: *What are we even trying to learn? Why does this even matter?*

So, let's make sure that you ask the hard questions up front. Let me show you how it's done.

What It Looks Like

A software development team within an international organization asked my team and me to help them think through how to improve one of their collaboration tools.

This team of engineers had built a proprietary collaboration software that operated like a big digital whiteboard. Team members from Alabama could draw on it and all their coworkers in Texas, Russia, and Germany could see what they were doing, as if it were happening on their own boards in real time.

They had written their own product specifications for this whiteboard. The tool had been tested. Everything was operating smoothly. There was only one problem: No one was using it.

The leader of the team started the conversation like this: "We've got some money set aside to further develop this tool, but people aren't utilizing it. We need to focus on fixing the product experience."

They were assuming the team wasn't using the software because of its user experience. They were also assuming that expanded functionality would move the whiteboard from its dormant position in the corner of the conference room to become a center-stage enabler of team collaboration and connection.

These were red flags for me. Something felt off in my gut.

"I think we need to take a step back," I told the software team. My intuition was telling me this wasn't a product issue. If it were, people would at least be trying to use the whiteboard, but they weren't. It was literally sitting in the corner, not plugged in. Few people had detailed feedback about the tool itself, just a unanimous position that what existed "wasn't working for them." And yet each person I spoke with was actively involved in creating the base requirements for what this tool should be and how it should work. And because they're all engineers, I was also pretty confident that nothing got lost in translation.

To say that my spidey senses were turned up is an understatement. The problem we were dealing with was not about the whiteboard tool; it was about workflow and process. Something about how the team did its work and interacted with one another didn't quite jive with this whiteboard device. This reflection is what set the focus of the research to come.

I told the team, "I think first and foremost we need to understand what collaboration means for your organization."

It was time for me to get curious. As I asked many questions of this team, I discovered that collaboration was becoming increasingly tricky. They were quickly expanding into new countries, bringing on additional team members, and encountering more cultural differences across these multiple agencies. The whiteboard had become a glorified solution to a growing sense of unease about collaboration, and ultimately workflow, considering this growth.

When the team approached me about this work, they defined the project as a product usability study. What we ended up conducting was a workflow process study, with the intent of understanding the following:

- What does collaboration mean to this organization?
- What does it look like?
- How and when does it show up?

By scaling out and making the project a workflow and process project, we uncovered that collaboration, in this team, happened when they were working independently, not together. The moments when they came together were moments of *negotiation*. Decisions on resourcing would be made in those connections, and then, outside that meeting, plans would be adjusted accordingly.

The digital whiteboard was trying to change a behavior of the team—to turn a moment of negotiation into one of collaboration, which just wasn't going to happen. That said, there were many opportunities identified to improve the collaborative workflow of the team.

We learned through the workflow and process analysis that this team used seven different systems in their work, with not even one of them integrating with the others. This caused a lot of rework for the team, with a high risk of errors due to manual data entry.

Ultimately, the money set aside to improve the idle whiteboard tool was diverted to further building out the seven other tools. As a result, collaboration improved significantly across this team.

Lead these conversations with a thirst for deeper understanding. **Seek to parse facts from assumptions.**

By leading the scoping process with curiosity and a healthy dose of skepticism, this team avoided spending time and money on a study that was too narrow in scope to offer them long-term value. Sure, we could have done a usability study on the digital whiteboard. I'm sure we could have developed new product specifications for that tool as well. Yet, none of this would have moved the needle on improving the team's real goal, which was to enable better collaboration across the team. A further build-out of the team's seven core systems, however, did just the trick!

Your Challenge: Accept Nothing at Face Value

Accepting nothing at face value is easier said than done, right? After all, while you're likely hearing about this problem or project for the very first time, your key stakeholders have been living or talking about it for quite a while.

Therefore, they'll likely come into this conversation confident not only about the problem itself, but also about what needs to be done to solve it successfully. They may define the solution pathway: "We need to improve the user experience of our product." Or dictate methodology: "We need to run focus groups with engineers at each key location of the organization."

This combination of stakeholder confidence paired with a predetermined solution pathway or methodology can result in you, the innovator, becoming an "order-taker"—reacting to what your stakeholders *say* they need instead of probing to understand what they *actually* need.

Stay vigilant, my friend. Take the posture of a question-asker rather than that of an order-taker. Ask the hard questions that will help you understand the real and underlying goals of the initiative.

Accept the Challenge:
Adopt an Inquiry-Based Project Scoping Script

As you enter your next scoping connection, I challenge you, innovator, to ask a lot more questions. Set aside the desire to be perceived as having it all figured out and trust the process of discovery. This isn't a sales pitch. You're not selling yourself in this conversation. You're genuinely trying to understand your stakeholders' needs so that you can design a project that will solve their real problem.

Lead these conversations with a thirst for deeper understanding. Seek to parse facts from assumptions. Here's a script that you can use to guide your next scoping conversation:

1   Have your project stakeholders communicate the project in their own words.

    Example question: Tell me about your project. I've read the Request for Proposal (RFP)/scoping document that you've shared and have some questions, but before we get there, tell me why we're here. What do you most want to learn or accomplish through this project?

2   Drill into the specifics of the project topic area and its connection to the broader organization.

    Example questions: What has led your team to focus on *this initiative* now? What business decision is the organization trying to make as a result of this work?

3   Explore the gaps in understanding, especially gaps that your stakeholder team perceives are holding them back from successful decision-making today.

    Example questions: What is holding you back from making that business decision today? What information or insight do you need that you currently don't have?

4   Identify what the "clarity outcome" looks like for your stakeholders.

Example question: How does gaining that information or insight help you and your team move forward toward your broader business goals?

Asking these questions—in this order—helps you to

- get your key stakeholders to share, in their own words, what they believe the project's scope is (they'll reveal more when they talk than when they write);

- connect the project to broader business goals and find out if there's any history that could impact the work—for better or worse;

- identify what's blocking clarity for the team;

- clarify how the project's outcomes will help stakeholders make more confident decisions. What will they be able to do that they can't do today?

I highly encourage you to engage in *live conversation* for this dialogue. Don't make this a form that you send to your stakeholders. Instead, treat your project-scoping connection like the qualitative, in-depth interview that it is. Lean in to probe the underlying beliefs impacting your innovation scope. Do you need a product usability test? Or are you better served with a workflow or process study, as was the case in the story I shared?

Pay attention to the details, stay fully engaged in the conversation, and probe the yellow and red flags that arise in the connection. Sometimes your stakeholders' preconceived solutions or methods are correct. But many times—*oftentimes*— they are not.

What to Expect

Calling bull on your stakeholders can be terrifying—especially if they're more senior to you. You might feel vulnerable going into this conversation, hesitant to ask the hard questions. You don't know them; they don't know you. They might question your knowledge, leadership, and capabilities. However, I urge you to move past your discomfort here. Your stakeholders will thank you and your project will be so much better when you do.

As humans, we naturally want to make ambiguous situations feel more concrete. So, we make declarative statements about solution pathways and methodologies as a way to feel more "in control" of the less-than-clear innovation challenge ahead of us. Your stakeholders are not trying to mislead you or the project. Most of the time, they haven't paused to recognize or question the assumptions they're presenting as facts.

This is where you come in. You turn off the autopilot. When you lean in with curiosity and probe with a healthy dose of skepticism, you walk away with a full understanding of what the team wants to accomplish. When you do this, you'll

- earn trust and credibility from your stakeholders;

- stay centered, grounded, and focused on the business decisions your work drives;

- scope the project to yield actionable insight that advances the business.

Mindset Shift: Accept Nothing at Face Value

Resist the urge to let your stakeholders lead the way. Yes, they're more familiar with the ins and outs of the problem. But they may be too embedded in it to see the forest for the trees. You know how to shape change-making processes to yield business impact. Be the question-asker rather than the order-taker in project scoping and kickoff to make sure you get real *actionable insight*.

2

Meet Your Stakeholders Where They Are

THE MAJORITY of organizations are *solution-focused* when it comes to innovation initiatives. What this means to you, as an innovator, is that your organization has rallied around launching a specific new offering into the market instead of solving a particular customer problem. This kind of focus on the solution (rather than the problem) has cascading impacts on the influence that you can have in your innovation work. It also means that the clock is ticking on delivering that new offering to the market for your stakeholders.

As an innovator, you face a choice: Advocate for pure research (to confirm the solution fits the market) or meet your stakeholders where they are (agreeing it's a good solution and helping to refine it for maximum impact). Managing this tension is no small task.

You know that taking the time to really understand the problem is best practice. You also know that rushing into things means you could miss some major blind spots along the way—blind spots that could ultimately impact the organization's long-term success in the market. Yet, you also empathize with your stakeholders' need for speed.

The time pressures your stakeholders feel are acute and only escalating. They have the "quick start" energy of bulls at the rodeo; they're raring and ready to go. If you ask them to step back and slow down, it might feel like you're cutting them off at the knees. The choice to advocate for process purity could be viewed as an obstacle to forward momentum, instead of the support it's intended to be. So, what do you do?

What It Looks Like

I was working with a city that was ranked as one of the worst cities for residential energy burden in the country. The majority of housing stock—from affordable housing to multimillion-dollar mansions—had not been built with energy efficiency in mind. Because of this, the average resident was spending more than double the national average of their monthly income on utilities, despite their region having the lowest per-unit energy rates of the nation.

The city team decided they wanted to address the residential energy burden of their community. They came up with a proposal: *Let's create a Groupon-type platform to aggregate purchasing demands for home-building materials.* The goal was to significantly reduce the costs for residents to retrofit or weatherize their homes. The hypothesis was this: If these homes were more energy-efficient, the city would significantly reduce their overall greenhouse gas emissions score. Success achieved!

I listened to the proposal, all while questioning its validity. To me, it seemed shortsighted and full of holes. But I knew approaching the team with judgement or suspicion wouldn't build trust or show my commitment to collaboration. Instead, I embraced the "Care Bear of love" energy that I mentioned in my opening chapter, "On the Runway." I leaned in with curiosity, seeking to understand why, from their perspective, this felt like *the right solution* for the residential energy burden crisis in their community. I asked the team to help me map out all of the assumptions behind the solution that they had identified.

Through this process, we pinpointed some fifty or more assumptions, but the two biggest (and most problematic, in my mind) were the following:

1   We assumed that the average city resident wanted to become a DIY expert. We weren't talking about small things like caulking windows; we meant large-scale projects such as replacing HVAC systems and installing new windows.

2   We assumed that building supply manufacturers wanted to work directly with consumers, despite this not being their typical business model. Historically, building supply manufacturers marketed to, sold to, and partnered with contractors who installed these products *for* residents.

Even though I suspected these assumptions would be major roadblocks, I was dealing with a team fixated on a specific solution and a tight six-month planning timeline tied to a grant that they were applying for. Pointing out all the issues and disrupting their plans right away wouldn't get me far. I needed to meet them where they were.

To that end, we designed the first "test" (of three) to answer the biggest assumptions shared above. The two questions centering that test were: *Does the average city resident want to become a DIY expert? Do building supply manufacturers want to work directly with consumers?*

To support that test, we created a concept statement for the solution: a description of what the solution was, how it worked, and who it was designed to support. We then gathered two different groups of people—residents and building supply manufacturers—to share this concept statement with. Within the first ten minutes of both meetings, it was clear that this Groupon-like platform would never have the impact desired.

The residents were pretty adamant that they had no intention of becoming DIY home improvement experts. They weren't going to install their own HVAC systems or windows, despite a lower cost on supplies. They said what they really needed was a way to find and hire trustworthy, vetted, and credentialed contractors committed to reducing the energy burden of their residential homes. They also voiced a desire for more certainty around which home improvement efforts, if embraced, would yield a significant and positive impact on their energy bills.

The building supply manufacturers also shared major concerns about the platform. They weren't interested in Joe Schmoe purchasing and installing their products—likely incorrectly. They felt that these erroneous installations would lead to negative marketing for the products and company, as people would take to bashing the product on social media, not accounting for the role they themselves might have played in the product not performing to expectation (if installed incorrectly). Yet, like residents, these building supply manufacturers also had a desire to connect with more trustworthy and reputable contractors.

Needless to say, that first test led to a major pivot for this team's solution. The information gained in that test made it clear that the root of the problem-to-solve was not access to affordable building materials. It had far more to do with helping people connect with contractors they could trust to help them make energy improvements to their homes that would yield results.

This pivot led the team to run two more tests to refine their platform's requirements. The second test focused on the belief that an energy audit alone wasn't enough to drive resident action. The goal was to figure out what would motivate residents to act on the energy-saving improvements suggested by the audit. Based on the results, the team created a new vision for the platform: a rewards-based system for encouraging behavioral change around residential energy consumption. This vision was then tested with residents in a third round of testing, receiving strong support.

Using the Test-and-Learn Approach to development helped me to meet my city stakeholders where they were at the start of this initiative. I didn't have to call out all the holes that I saw in their idea at that time (and make them feel bad about themselves in the process, or worse, dampen the excitement that they had about their project). I simply had to guide them to have their market (residents and building supply manufacturers) tell them what was working and what was not about that idea, so they could adapt and build based on that feedback.

Not only did the idea grow, but the team did as well—in their knowledge and application of innovation and in their purpose. One team member reflected at the end of the project, "In the current system, there is no incentive for a contractor to install an energy-efficient HVAC system, for instance. And our residents are not demanding that they do. Our platform is now driving energy efficiency demand."

While this team did not ultimately win the grant that they were competing for at the time, they did emerge from this effort changed and more committed than ever to being more resident-centric in how they approached innovation citywide.

Ask stakeholders where else in the development process they can save time, so you and your team can focus on doing things "right" up front.

Your Challenge:
Embrace a Test-and-Learn Approach

When working with *solution-focused* teams, you need to make a call from the start: Do you meet your stakeholders where they are and commit to helping them shape their new offering for maximum impact (as I did in the case study that I just shared with you)? Or do you champion a pure process and do some initial discovery research to ensure that the defined solution is indeed the right solution? There's no hard-and-fast rule on this one, only a trade-off to consider.

What's the risk to the business if you overlook a major blind spot? If the project is tied to an organization's flagship offering, it might be wise to push for a more thorough process. You don't want to jeopardize the company's long-term financial stability by building the wrong next offering. In such cases, ask stakeholders where else in the development process they can save time, so you and your team can focus on doing things "right" up front—investing in discovery research and fully understanding the problem before jumping to solutions.

If, however, the offering is not a flagship one or a marked growth initiative for the organization, then maybe you can bend in your advocacy of "pure process" and meet your stakeholders where they are, leaning more into a Test-and-Learn Approach for this offering's development. A Test-and-Learn Approach gives you insight into how to shape your solution to deliver maximum impact, but it does it through pressure testing the solution itself rather than up-front discovery research.

This approach likely goes against everything you've been taught to do. It's not on process. In fact, it circumvents the process. Some might even consider it "bad research." But the alternative—not doing any research at all—is a riskier proposition. You might solve the wrong problem. You might not solve any problem at all. You might get this thing out in the market and discover it has no value, but now there's no room to pivot. Yes, pursuing a Test-and-Learn Approach is off process, but if you take an either/or perspective here (either we do this perfectly on process or we don't do it at all), there won't be any research, and everyone loses in this game.

Alternatively, by taking a both/and approach (starting with the solution while doing research along the way), you can collaborate with your stakeholders to refine the solution as it develops, even within their time constraints. This method de-risks the project over time and increases its chances of success at market launch.

Accept the Challenge: Shape Solutions for Maximum Impact

When embracing a Test-and-Learn Approach, you're acknowledging up front that people have a vested interest in a specific solution. You're also accepting that your role is to help them optimize and de-risk that solution to ensure its best chance at success in the market. A Test-and-Learn Approach includes two key activities: an Assumptions Workshop, where key assumptions are identified, and iterative testing sprints aimed at validating or refining those assumptions.

The Assumptions Workshop, which typically takes three to four hours, is a series of exercises that uncover all the assumptions, both explicit and implicit, related to whatever the team is developing. It can be run on any new offering in the creation process—product or service.

Prior to the workshop itself, all stakeholder participants are assigned homework to complete. That homework has two parts: Create a five-panel storyboard for the new thing being created and choose an image that conveys what you hope this new offering will look and feel like to the people who will use it. The goal of these two homework assignments is to get "under the hood" on how people see this new offering coming to life in the world (i.e., who uses it, what problem it's helping to solve, how it works, and the impact it will have on people's everyday lives).

You then help the team—either before or during the workshop—to explicitly state the assumptions that emerge about the new offering through that homework assignment. For example, "We assume that the average city resident wants to become a DIY expert." Then, you lead people through a mapping exercise of all these assumptions, putting each one on a two-by-two diagram (see below). Keep in mind, this mapping exercise can take a while, considering most initiatives usually have fifty or more embedded assumptions.

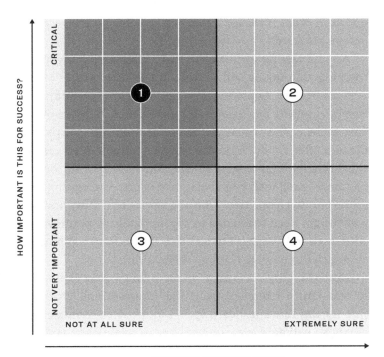

HOW SURE ARE YOU OF THIS?

One axis represents how critical the assumption is to the success of the project. The other axis represents how certain the participants are that the assumption is true. Any assumption that lands in the "critical" to the success of the project, yet uncertain—or "not at all sure"—about the truth of that assumption quadrant becomes the focus of your Test-and-Learn Sprints.

When designing the Test-and-Learn Sprints on the basis of those assumptions, it's important to recognize that *you're not building or piloting the solution itself.* Your goal is to uncover whether the core and critical assumptions currently guiding the development of that offering are accurate. This usually begins with very low-fidelity prototyping techniques, like card sorts, storyboards, or concept posters. In the early stages of your Test-and-Learn Approach, you're trying to answer the question *What is the idea, and is it of value for the people it's designed to serve?*

As your testing sprints evolve, the complexity of your prototyping techniques will as well. In the latter stages of your Test-and-Learn Approach, you're answering questions like, *How does it work and what will it do?* In each iteration of your Test-and-Learn Sprints, you're connecting with people who the new offering is designed to support, ultimately co-creating the definition of that solution with those people. At the completion of each test, you check in. Are the core assumptions underpinning your new offering correct? If not, how and what might need to change to appropriately respond? As you witnessed in "What It Looks Like," sometimes big pivots in approach can emerge through these sprints!

Note: I highly encourage you to engage your client team in this entire exercise, from the Assumptions Workshop through the Test-and-Learn Sprints to the after-sprint debriefs. Doing so will help everyone get on the same page and walk in lockstep with one another throughout the development process. This collaborative approach also prevents pushback and tension, as development teams can hear firsthand what's working and what's not. They can also be inspired on what tweaks to make to elevate value for the individuals the product is designed to serve.

What to Expect

Embracing the Test-and-Learn Approach is likely to be harder for you than it will be for your stakeholders, as this methodology requires you to let go of the purity of the research process and perhaps your own attachment to perfectionism. For some innovations, it can feel like Plan B. You might, at times, wonder if you're bastardizing the research process. You have to let all that go.

This approach, while different, is effective. It forces team conversations that generally don't happen throughout the development process and, in turn, brings newfound consciousness to the decisions made in the development of the new offering. In the short term, you end up with a new offering better positioned for market success. In the long term, you amplify your credibility as a professional and build trust and belief in research within your client organization.

What's important to underscore is that your stakeholders are likely going to *love* this approach to research and development. One of the biggest complaints that stakeholders have of innovation (and research-oriented teams) is the time it takes to do the up-front work. They feel stalled or held back in their development plans for months. This is even more acutely felt when a stakeholder team is working in a *solution-focused* work culture.

In a solution-focused environment, your stakeholders are committed to launching a new offering into the market, not to solving a problem. So, the idea of taking time to fall in love with the problem feels like wasted time and effort. Now, we all know that bad products make for bad business, but when management is bearing down on your stakeholders with aggressive launch timelines, "getting something out the door" is the mantra that is dominant in their conscience. Calling the new offering a minimum viable product (MVP) is how they alleviate their anxieties around whether they've built a good new offering or not.

I want you, innovator, to think of the Test-and-Learn Approach as the opportunity to support your stakeholders to fail forward. Give them opportunities to fail fast and the opportunity to rebound and pivot as needed. Help them clarify their MVP's essential features by developing it with real and iterative market feedback.

Mindset Shift: Embrace a Test-and-Learn Approach

Your job is to reduce the risk and increase the chances of success for the solution. You can do this by meeting teams where they are, guiding them to surface their assumptions, and to do iterative testing. You'll build stronger partnerships, more credibility, and a greater belief in research—paving the way for greater agility in the short term and more innovation in the long term.

3

Slay Energy Vampires

WE'VE ALL HAD those projects that feel like they're moving at the pace of "two steps forward, one step back." The inertia and lack of traction can feel mind-numbing, frustrating, exhausting... One thing is for sure: Joy disappears as the project unfolds, and the team is left feeling drained and disheartened instead of fueled up and inspired.

Sure, you might get to the end of that project with a "successful" outcome (i.e., a victorious new product launch, increased revenue or profit for the company), yet your personal experience throughout the process is one you'd prefer to forget. I often refer to these projects as "Energy Vampires." A typical innovation initiative is months long, not just hours or days. That level of sustained, drained energy and weight takes its toll. It doesn't just affect that one project; it comes with cascading impacts, influencing other projects you might be managing, your health, your relationships, and more.

I want you to feel empowered to slay the Energy Vampires before they happen—if not all of them, then at least as many as you can. (Heaven knows, there are enough *free fall* moments in a project: moments you can't predict or plan for, but that you still need to move through with grace and grit. But that's coming in Part 2, "Free Fall.") This chapter is about helping you to preemptively identify and deal with the Energy Vampires, the obstacles, and challenges that can be foreseen in your project.

What this looks like in practice is creating the habit of thinking about all the ways your project could go sideways *before* the project starts. You get bonus points if you do this exercise as a team and bring a touch of snark and cynicism to the table when you have these discussions.

What It Looks Like

We had just been hired to support a healthcare organization to create its digital strategy. An important nuance of this project was that the company had recently acquired several new entities, all of which were using different digital platforms. Sylver Consulting was brought in to help develop a unified digital strategy that all entities could execute together.

When my team sat down to do our Energy Drain Assessment for the project, we surfaced a number of potential concerns—project dynamics that, if left unchecked, could slow the project's momentum:

- The initiative involved about thirty stakeholders due to its focus and reach across multiple entities within the organization.

- These entities had little experience, up to this point, in collaborating effectively with one another.

- While they *wanted* an integrated digital strategy, the organization had yet to define the performance metrics needed to support it.

In short, I was worried there were "too many cooks in the kitchen" in this initiative, each with different goals. I was also coming off a particularly traumatic project that had similar circumstances and dynamics to this one. The timeline of that recent initiative had tripled due to having "too many cooks in the kitchen." As its timeline kept dragging on, stakeholders stopped waiting for the results before making key business decisions, which severely lessened the impact of that work. The timeline delays also caused major resourcing challenges for my team. I was determined to avoid a repeat of that experience on this project.

Hence, I advocated for defining a stakeholder engagement strategy. It was clear that we needed input from all thirty stakeholders. Each brought valuable context about their current digital strategy and insights on what was practically and legally feasible in an integrated approach. But if we didn't have clarity on the roles and responsibilities across the team and alignment on how decisions were going to be made, this project was likely to become an Energy Vampire.

We all know who slays a vampire: A stake-holder! So, I gave responsibility assignments to every stakeholder—using the RACI model:

- **Responsible Stakeholders** were the core team members, like me, and were responsible for doing the work.

- **Accountable Stakeholders** were three people—lead representatives from each of the organization's key divisions, who were responsible for making final decisions on the work's scope.

- **Consulted Stakeholders** were the many other team members (approximately twenty-seven), who were being asked to provide input, feedback, or expertise before any final decisions were made or actions taken.

- **Informed Stakeholders** were the people that the team committed to keeping in the loop about the progress and decisions but were not involved in project execution or decision-making.

In addition to clarifying project roles, we also established a four-phased approval process for key deliverables:

- Phase 1 involved my team meeting with our primary contact for the project and other Responsible Stakeholders. They would review the milestone deliverable, provide feedback, and we'd make the necessary edits based on their input.

- Phase 2 involved sharing the updated version of the milestone deliverable with the Consulted Stakeholders. We'd gather their feedback and, based on the discussion, make further edits or adjustments as needed.

- Phase 3 involved meeting with Accountable Stakeholders from each division to get the final approval on the milestone deliverable.

- Phase 4 had Responsible and Accountable Stakeholders providing updates to Informed Stakeholders on project progress as they deemed necessary.

This clarity on stakeholder roles and responsibilities was a game changer for this project, compared to the prior one that I mentioned. Having a defined stakeholder-engagement strategy made all the difference to keeping this project on timeline and on budget. The Energy Vampire was slain before it could even show up. Moreover, each of the company divisions came out of this engagement with greater appreciation for what might be enabled in their respective verticals if they truly collaborated in the creation of an integrated digital strategy. The project was a great success!

The Energy Vampire was slain before it could even show up.

Your Challenge: Plan for the Energy Sucks

The goal of this exercise is to plan, *in advance,* for different energy drains that you could foresee disrupting your project, factors that could negatively impact your timeline, budget, and outcomes. For example, think about your project sample and how easy or hard it might be to find those folks. Consider who needs to be involved from an approval point of view, to advocate for next steps as a result of the work. Consider your project goals and whether you need to clarify any terms or intentions about those goals.

You literally want to itemize every potential energy suck—big or small—that might negatively impact your ability to execute the project with *ease* and actionability, within the proposed timeline and budget. You do this so that you can collectively assess what to do about each energy drain identified *before* it becomes the weak link that threatens to undermine your project's success.

In some cases, there's something you can do now to mitigate or eliminate those foreseen energy sinks. For instance, if you're worried about getting buy-in for the outcomes of your work, how might you engage those key stakeholders in meaningful ways throughout the project? You might adjust attendee lists for certain meetings or add additional checkpoints into the calendar.

In other cases, you just have to wait and see if the energy drain, as you've predicted it, actually becomes a reality. I often find this to be true when we discuss participant samples. For instance, when we quote studies, we need to make a "best guess" on incidence rate (the percentage of people who would likely qualify for inclusion in our study). Sometimes our projections are accurate and other times they're not. But we can't know how accurate they are until we start fielding.

Regardless of whether we choose to address the energy sucks identified in the moment or not, surfacing them and bringing them into the consciousness of the project team is powerful. The entire team can then keep an eye out for this energy sink in the project and, because you've already put voice to this potential obstacle, your subconscious will make contingency plans on how to address it should it show up. Some people might argue that, by speaking the energy drain out loud, you might be speaking it into being. That's not been my experience. In general, I've found that this practice has more return rewards than drawbacks.

Accept the Challenge: Facilitate an Energy Drain Assessment

The most difficult part of this challenge (at least for me personally) is assuming the Debbie Downer posture necessary to foresee potential problems in your initiative. I much prefer to orient toward life with a positive and optimistic lens. The Debbie Downer persona encourages you to view your project and the execution environment through a pessimistic lens. Entering this negative headspace gives you a gut punch that doesn't feel super great in the moment. It can pique anxiety for a bit. It can certainly drain your own energy. However, all of this is done in service of preventing the long and sustained drain of a project that's off-timeline and exceeding budget.

How do you do this? I suggest following a three-step process:

1   Create an Energy Drain Assessment Matrix for your project, using Microsoft Excel or Google Sheets. Create that matrix with five key columns:

Column A: Energy drains that you can foresee disrupting your project.

Column B: The potential impact of those energy drains on your initiative. Assign a 1–3 rating for each obstacle identified. (1 = likely to have a minimal impact on the project's timeline, budget, and/or outcome; 3 = could have a major impact on the project's timeline, budget, and/or outcome.)

Column C: A question: Do you need to take immediate action to mitigate or eliminate this energy drain? Yes or no.

Column D: What next step actions will be taken (now or in the future).

Column E: Any other contextual insight that is valuable to capture about that potential energy drain.

2   Then, go to town on voicing—out loud—all the key energy drains that you can foresee popping up during project execution. Invite your team and maybe even your key stakeholders into this dialogue, with each of you identifying (based on the lens of your own functional role) the ways that your project might go sideways. I suggest doing this step independently, each filling out Columns A and B on the Energy Drain Assessment Matrix. Get every potential energy suck that can be foreseen out on the table—big or small.

3   Then, come together to discuss each key energy drain defined, starting with those with a 3 rating, then 2, and finally 1. The goal of the discussion is to align on what actions, if needed, the team should take to mitigate or eliminate that project energy suck, as well as when those interventions should be taken—immediately or possibly at a later point in time. (Complete Columns C to E in the spreadsheet.)

The value of this discussion is that it gets everyone on the same page, seeing the project from the vantage point of all key execution partners. You're also then equipped to execute your project with greater ease and actionability; you have meta-phorically—and preemptively—slayed the Energy Vampire of a project gone sideways.

What to Expect

Taking the time to do this Energy Drain Assessment up front can be challenging. From an inner perspective, you might rebel... who really *wants* to be a Debbie Downer? Not I! You also might not feel comfortable inviting your full execution team or key stakeholders into the exercise. *Do you really want to encourage thoughts on what might not work about what you've got planned before you even start? Might your competence as a leader be questioned?* These can be the fears—legitimate or not—that roll around in your head.

But before you dismiss this activity, before you consciously decide to not execute this activity on your next initiative, bring into view those past projects that have sucked you of joy. Remember those projects that had gone awry, the ones where a timeline was wishful thinking at best or where you felt like you were spending money hand over fist to mitigate problems that you didn't foresee.

This exercise creates a safe space of dialogue between you, your team, and your stakeholders. The simple act of bringing potential energy sinks into the light reduces their power to undermine effective execution of your project. In some cases, you might choose to take new action in the moment to miti-gate a foreseen obstacle. In others, you'll choose a "let's wait and see" approach. Regardless, you're inviting more people into the "watch squad" related to these potential energy sucks, thus reducing the weight on your own shoulders to have it all figured out.

I do advocate that you plan for the energy drains in *every* project that you take on. You can play with the formality of how you choose to execute it (i.e., do you spreadsheet all the energy drains or not?). But I don't recommend that you consider it optional. Doing so puts your personal joy at risk... something I don't want you to do.

For us at Sylver Consulting, the larger projects get the spreadsheeted Energy Drain Assessment. For smaller initiatives, we have iterative energy drain dialogues throughout the project, but don't go as far as formalizing those foreseen energy sucks into an Excel spreadsheet.

Bottom line, I invite you to figure out what works best for you, innovator, but don't consider this step optional. Also, don't lose sight of its purpose, which is to protect your joy!

Mindset Shift: Plan for the Energy Sucks

A couple of hours of scrutinizing your project and projecting where and how it could fail can offer tenfold returns to its execution. Embrace your inner Debbie Downer and invite your team and key stakeholders to do the same. Voice all the ways that your project could go sideways, so that you can plan ahead on how to respond to foreseen energy drains on your project. Then, relish how you've set yourself up for a more easeful, joyful, and effective project experience.

4

Define Project Success

MAYA ANGELOU famously said, "People will forget what you said, people will forget what you did, but people will never forget how you made them feel." Believe it or not, this applies perfectly to an innovation process as well. People might forget what you said, the details of the process, or the journey they took along the way, but they won't forget the results or how the process made them feel. That will stick with them and be a barometer for whether the project was a "good" one or a "bad" one, after the fact.

That's why it's so important to be aligned, at the start, on what project success really means for you and your stakeholders. You need to articulate, from the beginning, what would leave a stakeholder team feeling 100 percent fulfilled by the project, versus simply satisfied or, worse, unsatisfied or disappointed.

You see, success is multidimensional. It encompasses both personal and group-oriented facets. It's also defined by more than societal definitions, such as return on investment (ROI) metrics or specific KPIs. For a project to be an outstanding success, it needs to leave the people engaged in it with a deep sense of fulfillment. This is only possible if you're able to tap into their hearts at the start of the project, to define what success really *looks like* and *feels like* for them, personally.

In other words, you, as an innovator, need to fully grasp the functional, logistical, emotional, social, and even spiritual needs of your project before getting started. And therein lies the problem: RFPs and project kickoffs lay out the functional and logistical needs (i.e., the technical requirements of the work) well enough, but almost never dig deep enough to articulate the emotional, social, and spiritual needs of the initiative. To truly support your stakeholders and ensure they feel fulfilled, you need the whole story. And, whether we like it or not, it is these emotional, social, and spiritual needs that ultimately drive that sense of fulfillment, far more than the functional and logistical needs that initially made it into the RFP.

Therefore, your challenge is to surface the full scope of needs underpinning the project—at the start of the project—so that you can use this knowledge to intentionally design the engagement journey of your initiative. In some cases, this might impact the overall methodology or approach. In other cases, it might simply influence the questions you choose to ask or discussions you choose to facilitate throughout the project.

Let me tell you about what it looks like to surface the full scope of needs around an initiative in a scoping call.

What It Looks Like

Sylver Consulting was working with a year-old startup at a critical point in its journey. The company needed to scale to more cities within the next year or face shutting down. In the short term, it needed to attract more customers and increase spending from its regulars to fuel growth.

As we started our conversation, the clients admitted they'd been focused entirely on operations so far. They sensed something wasn't right with their marketing but couldn't pinpoint the issue. They suspected they were missing key insights about their ideal customer—insights they believed qualitative research could help illuminate.

As I listened, I took note. The client had already identified the functional and logistical needs of the project. They wanted to define their ideal customer and believed a qualitative approach would be the best way to gather the meaningful insights they needed for their business.

I could have stopped there in the conversation. I was crystal clear on what the client needed to do and their expectations on methodology (and agreed with their assessment). But, instead, I decided to press more, and asked, "What do you *not* want to have happen going through or coming out of this project?"

My client paused. "No one has ever asked me that before. What an interesting question! I don't want insights that are too general that I don't know how to act on them."

Excellent, I thought. I probed more: "What is a type of insight that might feel 'too general' to you?"

She thought about it. "I'm not sure where we're more stuck in the marketing funnel—in awareness or conversion. I hope this project will help me to answer that."

Interesting, I thought. The project that we had been talking about, up to this point, would not answer this question for her. The conversation, so far, had painted the picture that we were most interested in defining what would support trial and loyalty for this ideal customer, not what was needed to gain potential awareness. I thought, *Great! I'm now collecting additional breadcrumbs on what will yield a truly successful project for this client.* (This specific tidbit of information led to an expansion in the project's methodology. We added a light quantitative study into the recruitment effort for the qualitative research to better understand performance metrics related to awareness and conversion.)

Now back to the questioning. I asked next, "How do you *not* want to feel going through or coming out of this initiative?"

She responded, "I don't want to feel like my team and I are speaking in different languages or like no one is on the same page."

As I probed deeper, I learned that the team had been experimenting with marketing quite a bit. They had done some social outreach analyses to identify which type of messaging or imagery seemed to be doing better than others. Yet, when it came to hypothesizing about why these results were as they were, everyone had different ideas to share. Getting everyone on the same page—all rowing in the same direction—was a social outcome that this project owner deeply hoped for. I knew now, based on this conversation, that we needed to engage not just the marketing director (whom I was speaking with) in this initiative, but also the marketing communications manager, the product manager, and the CEO. The team roster for this project was coming together.

I then asked the third question of the five that will infallibly help you define the full scope of needs around a project: "What do you want to have happen during or as a result of this project?"

The client spoke of her love of consumer research and how her history as a P&G marketer had shown her, over and over, the power of good consumer research. She had seen, time and again, how clarity on who you're targeting leads to a clearer and more precise strategy, which in turn produces more predictable results. She wanted engagement in this project to quench her emotional thirst for research. I knew, then, that I needed a collaborative engagement strategy around this project that would support this client to feel like she had "gotten her hands dirty" in the process—in a good way!

I followed up with the fourth question: "How do you want to feel going through or coming out of this initiative?"

She responded, "I want to feel curious and excited by what my team and I are learning."

Her expression of this emotional need helped to validate my thoughts on the collaborative engagement strategy for the initiative.

I then asked the final question—the one that surfaced the marketing director's deep spiritual need for validation: "How do you want others to feel?"

She broke open. "People think they understand everything about marketing, that it's so easy. I hope this project helps my colleagues truly *see* and *understand* the full value of marketing and why this part of the company's go-to-market strategy deserves the same level of investment as others."

Bingo! This project was not just about the immediate initiative in front of us. This project was also meant to be a catalyst of *culture change* that would help support her in her functional marketing role, to rise in credibility and significance within the organization. This point just further underscored the importance of involving the marketing communications manager, product manager, and CEO in the initiative and the need for that collaborative engagement strategy.

Bottom line: This targeted dialogue helped to bring shape and direction to the study that we proposed and executed for this client. Had we not had it, we would not have added the quantitative component to the methodology that I mentioned earlier. We also would have foregone the suggestion of a Sensemaking Workshop at the end of the project, due to budget constraints around the initiative. However, this conversation highlighted just how important it was for this project owner

As an innovation leader, you're managing more than just projects—you're also managing anxieties.

to bring her colleagues along in the journey. Thus, that Sensemaking Workshop became a nonnegotiable piece of the collaborative engagement journey that guided this initiative. And the result is a project that has delivered significant ROI for the organization.

One year out from this initiative, the organization has developed a multipronged and cross-functional marketing strategy that has helped it to achieve its business goals for this initiative:

- more customers
- more "share of wallet" from its regular customers
- expansions into new geographic territories

I recently spoke to the CEO. He communicated, with a sigh of relief, "We have finally unlocked growth. Your research undoubtedly played a significant role in that. Thank you!"

Your Challenge:
Surface All Needs of Your Project

Your responsibility as an innovation leader—at the start of an initiative—is to define the range of functional, logistical, emotional, social, and spiritual needs of that project. Yes, I know, this is a big ask. It might even start to feel "touchy-feely" to some, but it's also nonnegotiable. As an innovation leader, you're managing more than just projects—you're also managing anxieties. That's right—an implicit part of your job description is to manage the anxiety of your stakeholders as they go through the transformative process that is innovation.

Anxiety is piqued in any individual when they're out of alignment—when what's happening in and around them is not aligned to what their soul really needs and craves. This misalignment might be described as feeling unsettled, nervous, worried, or anxious. A stakeholder in this state might feel like something is "off" in how you've scoped the project or how the project is unfolding, but they don't know how to articulate what that "offness" really is. There's just a general sense of restlessness that lingers beneath the surface.

If left unchecked, that restlessness, that misalignment will come back to bite your project in the butt, in the form of poor decision-making and avoidance behaviors. In contrast, if you surface the anxieties from the start and continually check in on them throughout your initiative, you pave the path for true creativity and innovation throughout. And you can support transformation in an authentic way.

Your challenge, therefore, is to surface all the potential negative anxieties, hopes, and dreams that your stakeholders might have in relation to your project, from the start. But let me be really clear—you're not a mind reader, nor should you pretend to be one. There's no way for you to know what a person wants or doesn't want *without asking*. Therefore, you must be willing to *put yourself out there* and ask some potentially weird, maybe even slightly vulnerable questions of your stakeholders to try to understand what their soul really wants and needs from the initiative you're about to embark on. You will likely tell yourself: *Maybe we should skip this step? I don't want to waste their time on this. The outcome needs around this project are clear enough.*

But are they? ... Really?

Accept the Challenge: Ask Five Intention-Setting Questions

You've now witnessed, through my story, the value of surfacing the full scope of needs underpinning your project. You saw how asking a few (insert: potentially weird and vulnerable) questions helped to round out the methodology used to structure the work scope of my startup client. How those same questions supported the creation of the engagement strategy for the full initiative and how they clarified who needed to be part of the project team. I call these questions the Five Intention-Setting Questions, adapted from Dominick's book, *Different: The Highly Sensitive Leadership Revolution.* They serve to create clarity around what success *looks like* and *feels like* for stakeholders in a project.

I want you to use these same questions in your work, so that you, too, can gain clarity on what the success of your project holistically looks like and feels like for your stakeholders. You want to ask these questions, in exactly this order; don't deviate:

1 What do you *not* want to have happen during or as a result of this project?

2 How do you *not* want to feel going through or coming out of this project?

3 What do you want to have happen during or as a result of this project?

4 How do you want to feel going through and coming out of this project?

5 How do you want others to feel?

The sequence of these questions is very important. Trust me—I know—you'll be tempted to reverse the order, to start with the positive questions before turning to the negative-toned ones. Don't do it!

The question flow is intentional. Starting with the negative-toned questions helps stakeholders acknowledge and release anxieties that cloud their judgement and block deeper engagement with the project. Giving participants the space to express their fears and concerns creates an opening for them to also fully express their hopes and dreams for the initiative. This act of discharging and releasing the negative emotions surrounding a project is what empowers the stakeholder team to define, with more nuance, what success *really looks like* and *feels like* to the organization, to the people they serve, and to themselves and their own personal transformation as they embrace the initiative that lies ahead.

As you listen, focus on how the project's scope aligns with the speaker's vision of success. Does anything need to change regarding the scope, methodology, execution, or support structures around the project to fully meet the functional, logistical, emotional, social, and spiritual needs your stakeholders are sharing with you? As these changes come to you, make note of them to refer back to later or call them out for further discussion in the moment—whatever feels right.

Notice, over time, how these questions give people permission to voice whatever comes to mind, the stuff they wouldn't put down on paper because it either feels like fluff or feels too audacious. These questions, and the space you hold when asking them, helps your stakeholders to clarify and make visible the full scope of needs that they have for the initiative. This, in turn, gives you all the information you need to design and execute a project that results in a sense of true fulfillment in the end.

I personally use these Five Intention-Setting Questions on *every* initiative—at the scoping call (as demonstrated in the story) and the project kickoff. At project scoping, answers to these questions help you design a project that will yield the outcomes most needed from the initiative. At kickoff, these questions serve to create a unified vision for what success looks like and feels like for the project—a vision of success that the whole team is aligned on and can return to throughout the project as needed to recenter and reground.

What to Expect

Leading a team through a handful of "touchy-feely" questions might feel weird and awkward. It does—initially. But the return for being brave and bold in the asking of these questions far exceeds the few moments of discomfort that you will feel.

I encourage you to push back on the internal or external voices that tell you people don't want to "waste their time" with this kind of stuff. Let go of the assumption that people are too busy to have this type of conversation. This is your fear talking. The twenty to thirty minutes you'll spend on this will save you—and the entire team—immeasurable time (and possible heartache) in the future. I promise.

Case in point, the marketing director I talked to in the case study above told me afterward, "I thought those questions you asked us at the start of the project were really cool and also a little weird. But now, at the end of the project, I can see how important each of those questions were to shaping the client engagement experience underneath this initiative. In everything, your team has met, and in many cases exceeded, our expectations. Thank you!"

This reflection really touches my soul, and I hope demonstrates for you, innovator, *why* you should ask these Five Intention-Setting Questions, even if you might consider them a bit woo-woo yourself.

You, innovator, are responsible for managing your client's experience around your project. Yes, that means getting the work done. But it is also about anxiety management. These questions give your stakeholders space to express their concerns, worries, apprehensions, or tensions around your project. It also supports them in voicing, with their full heart, their hopes and wishes for the initiative.

Armed with this info, you're well positioned to deliver an *experience journey* around your project that supports your stakeholders to feel 100 percent heard and acknowledged. This makes them feel safe and, in turn, motivated... all of which manifests as good aligned, collaborative energy that serves as rocket fuel for your initiative.

Mindset Shift: Surface All Needs of Your Project

Remember, your role as an innovation leader is to manage the overall feeling of the project. To do that well, you need to understand the full scope of needs underpinning your project—the functional, logistical, emotional, social, and spiritual needs. The Five Intention-Setting Questions help to surface these needs, giving you the roadmap for how to deliver *success*—holistically and predictably—for your clients.

5

Clarify Innovation Ambition

W E'VE ALL HEARD more than a couple of stories of consulting companies taking on a project and running with it, only to come back with fantastic, groundbreaking ideas that the hiring organization could do absolutely nothing with. The research, documents, and prototypes are shelved, and everyone leaves the situation resentful. The hiring organization feels they didn't get the value they deserved for the price tag they paid. The consulting firm feels as if their efforts were undervalued and that the client wasn't nearly as progressive as it had hoped.

Does each party in this scenario have a right to feel slighted? Perhaps. But the true lesson here is that the two parties weren't working towards a common goal.

The term "innovation"—along with its shopworn adjective "innovative" and its breathless verb "innovate!"—has become the rallying cry of every product manager, the pursuit of every design consultant, the autocomplete of every press release writer. The word has been wrapped around everything from the newest, net-new offering (Apple iPod, Uber, the Nest) to a new template in Microsoft Word, and everything in between. Technically, innovation is simply something new; there are no qualifiers of how groundbreaking or world-shattering something needs to be. And that's where the trouble starts.

When an organization requests innovation as an outcome of their work, exactly what are they requesting?

Getting to the bottom of this question is your job, dear innovator. This chapter is a rallying cry for you, urging you to bring your stakeholders together to define the *type of innovation* outputs expected of your initiative.

Let's parse what this means...

What It Looks Like

My company, Sylver Consulting, was working with a direct sales organization. Their RFP said they wanted to develop a new winning product line that would bring market leadership back to the brand. Contextually, this organization was going through a lot of personnel change. They had recently hired a number of new people with the intent to challenge the organization to think differently and dream big. Our stakeholder team included people who were new to the organization along with some who had significant tenure. This team makeup was intentional, handpicked to ensure that we were conscious of all the business model guardrails—spoken and latent—that might impact our success.

We kicked off the initiative with a three-hour Setting the Stage for Success workshop. The first exercise of that workshop was to define the innovation ambition for our project. Before setting the scope, we needed to understand the company's overall stance on innovation. The full project team, consisting of six key stakeholders, attended, and each participant completed a short homework assignment tailored to their tenure with the organization.

We asked tenured employees to reflect on instances where the company had said no to innovation, either directly to them or to others. For each situation, they were tasked with giving it a title, describing the event, noting the explicit reasons for the rejection, and identifying any unspoken or implicit reasons they believed were at play. Finally, they were asked to consider what the no revealed about the company's overall stance on innovation and its tolerance for risk.

For new stakeholders, we asked them to compare the innovation culture of a previous employer to that of their current organization—the direct sales company sponsoring the work. They were prompted to answer these questions: *What similarities exist between the two cultures? What differences stand out? How was your previous employer more open to innovation? And in what ways was it more closed to innovation?*

We began the workshop by unpacking people's responses to the homework. Historically, we learned that the organization had gone through a tough time and had responded to that season in their business by pulling back on all innovation investments. The company was thankfully no longer in dire straits and had hopes of returning to a place of innovation leadership (which was good for our project). However, the trauma of that time loomed large for leaders and created important guardrails for our initiative. This company was more likely to say yes to new innovations that might emerge from our work if the new products proposed were globally relevant, could be manufactured in-house, and aligned to the current sales approaches of their sales force.

With these guardrails in hand, we turned to Part 2 of the Defining Innovation Ambition exercise. We needed alignment on the type of innovation output desired from the work. Was the team looking for outputs that would help them better *compete* with others in their category? Did they want to *play the game better* than they were today, looking for more adjacent products and assets to bring into their portfolio? Or were they really looking to *change the game* of their industry, being open to exploring wholly new products or assets that might respond to new customer needs and targets not yet addressed by their organization?

We asked each team member to place an orange star on the following Innovation Ambition Matrix (an adaptation of Bansi Nagji and Geoff Tuff's matrix in their *Harvard Business Review* article, "Managing Your Innovation Portfolio").

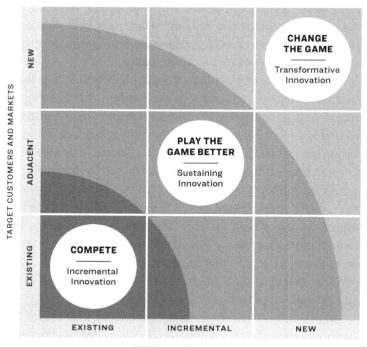

The newer members of the team immediately, and quite confidently, placed their stars in the "Change the Game" space of the graph. The tenured employees were more tentative. They took their time placing their stars and, with hesitancy, eventually settled on the middle ground between "Play the Game Better" and "Change the Game."

There was a good reason for this emerging ambition split. Everyone knew leadership had designed and sanctioned this initiative to be different from previous attempts at innovation. They had told the project team to "shoot for the stars." Furthermore, leadership had brought the new people into the organization with the intention of shaking things up. And so, after a thirty-minute discussion, the team finally committed to the "Change the Game" position, but noted, as they were doing so, that they would need to tightly manage some constraints along the way. There was concern among the more tenured employees that the reality of the "shoot for the stars" directive would be more restrictive than the team was initially being led to believe ... as ultimately proved to be the case.

Your Challenge:
Define the Appetite for Innovation

A team's appetite for innovation is defined based on their *motivation* and *tolerance* for innovation in that moment. From a motivation perspective, corporations typically seek innovation services in response to one of three situations:

1   They're currently engulfed in the flames of the "burning platform" (as my long-time mentor Russ Ward calls it). Their profits are dropping, their products aren't selling, and they don't know what to do about it.

2   They've emerged from the days of the burning platform and have come to understand that innovation is not a start/stop process, but an evolving one that requires constant attention.

3   They're a leader in their industry and determined to stay there. Failure is accepted within their organization because they understand and fully embrace the numbers game in product development.

Each of these situations generates a different tolerance around innovation within the organization.

1   Companies engulfed in the flames of a burning platform are often seeking innovation in a reactive mode. Speed is of the utmost concern and innovation often means taking the "me-too" approach in response to competitors. Organizations like this are often open to incremental innovation, with the ambition of better competing in the market. They're looking to optimize existing products, services, or offerings and want to take on very little risk while doing it.

2   Organizations that have recently emerged from the days of the burning platform are focused on quick hits and small wins. While they're thankful they've found some stability, the days of job insecurity are too close for them to feel comfort in thinking "blue sky." They're often looking for "Sustaining Innovation" outputs—new market pathways that help them "Play the Game Better." This might include improving the offerings they currently have, or it could entail creating something net-new. Their innovation ambition, in this case, is driven by their desire to secure or establish their market position by creating additional value in their offerings. They want their offerings to address existing unmet needs in the market or among their customer base. In this case, their risk tolerance is medium.

A team's appetite for innovation is defined based on **their *motivation* and *tolerance* for innovation in that moment.**

3   Industry leaders usually have time—and the benefits of
positive cash flow—on their side. They can think strategically about where they are today and where they want to be
in the future. They still need the small wins, but they can
afford to think more tactically about how those successes
contribute to a larger corporate strategy. These tend to be
the organizations open to "Transformative Innovation."
They want to "Change the Game" of their industry. They
no longer wish to compete on value. Rather, they want to
define the new bar of value and they're willing to take on
greater risk to do it.

Accept the Challenge: Align on Your Project's Innovation Ambition

This activity of defining your project's innovation ambition
has two key parts: Part 1 is about fostering a conversation
related to your organization's posture towards innovation.
Part 2 is about getting the full project team to align on the type
of innovation output they want to see.

There's no one "perfect" question to ask when facilitating
that Part 1 conversation. In the case of my client, we used two
different prompts, due to the varying tenures of the people on
the team. For quick reference, those two prompts were the
following:

- Reflect on the times when the company told you no for an
innovation idea (or when you've seen others being told no).

- Do a brief comparison of the innovation culture at a former employer to the innovation culture of your current
employer.

The goal of the Part 1 discussion is to support storytelling around past innovation initiatives so that the team can collectively process the organization's innovation readiness and risk tolerance. I encourage you to be creative with how you choose to spark the telling of those stories.

After discussing past postures towards innovation, it's time to declare your project's Innovation Ambition. I suggest printing the Innovation Ambition Matrix in a large format (there is a free downloadable resource of it on the website for this book). Give each team member a star sticker or voting dot and ask them to place it in the square that best represents the innovation outcome they hope to achieve from this project.

Once everyone has placed their individual vote, lead a discussion about why people put their vote in the squares they chose. The goal of this conversation is to decide, together, which square (or squares) represent the desired output focus for the current initiative.

Where the team casts its final vote will shape every decision moving forward. This will affect whom you involve in the research, what you ask of them, how you brainstorm new solutions, and how you measure success. So, don't rush this part. Give it the time and attention it needs and keep coming back to it as a guide throughout the project.

I also *highly recommend* that you do this exercise with *all key stakeholders* at the kickoff of your project. Much like the Five Intention-Setting Questions shared in chapter 4, the public nature of this discussion holds team members accountable to these ambitions for innovation as you move through the initiative.

What to Expect

If you do this right, you and your team will emerge from this discussion aligned on your innovation ambition. You'll experience a kumbaya-type moment where everyone feels harmoniously unified in the outputs of your project, which is *very good*. Yet, I want to wave a red flag of caution for you. This conversation around innovation ambition is not a one-and-done type of deal. The poster output of this exercise is a wonderful asset for you and the project, a visual reference to bring your team back to at iterative points in your initiative.

It's not uncommon, for instance, for stakeholders to boomerang back into what feels comfortable to them as they move through the innovation journey. For instance, the stakeholders in my story said they wanted to create "Change the Game" innovations from our work. Yet, once we got to ideation, they were prioritizing innovations that had tones of "Compete" and "Play the Game Better" over other *transforming* "Change-the-Game" innovations.

Having their Innovation Ambition Matrix as a reference helped my team and me facilitate heartfelt conversations with them. Did they really want to make the choices they were making, or did they want to stretch themselves a bit further than their natural inclinations were allowing in the moment?

In the end, the team pitched several new products for development that hit in that mid-space of innovation, between "Change the Game" and "Play the Game Better"—just as the tenured employees had anticipated. However, I'm not sure that we would have landed there without the Innovation Ambition Matrix to keep us focused and accountable to our goals throughout the project.

Mindset Shift: Define the Appetite for Innovation

Technically, innovation is simply introducing something new; there are no qualifiers of how groundbreaking or world-shattering it needs to be. Help your stakeholders clarify the type of innovation they're aiming for at the start of your initiative. Do they want the outcomes of your work to position them to "Change the Game" of their industry? To help them "Play the Game Better?" Or to just help them "Compete" better than they do today? Define this up front, so that you can more predictably deliver the results the organization is prepared to act upon.

6

Use Past Experiences to Direct the Future

NNOVATION in some organizations is a dirty word, met with eye rolls and dismissive commentary: "We've done this project before and it didn't work because [x, y, z]. How is this going to be any different?"

Comments like this make my skin crawl. I want to scream, "The past does not *have to* predict the future, people!" And yet, past trauma, related to innovation, is real. And it does impact how your stakeholders choose to show up for you in your current project. This is a fact.

So, what do you do about it?

You can push through, attempting to avoid this fact. Or you can address past innovation trauma head-on. I recommend the latter approach.

When your stakeholder team has unresolved innovation *baggage,* they will bring unhealthy and unproductive emotional weight into your initiative, which manifests as anxiety, fear, self-doubt, avoidance, or distorted thinking. Your goal is to unburden the team of this emotional weight—to share its load across the team—so that you can mitigate the impacts of that past *baggage* on your upcoming project. And this is all done in service of turbo-boosting the output of your upcoming initiative.

What It Looks Like

The team and I at Sylver Consulting were facilitating an innovation summit for a pet food brand. This was the seventh annual summit event, a time when key leaders of the organization came together to ideate new potential products for their pipeline. The goal of the summit was to create several new ideas that they would then further vet, develop, and scope, ultimately resulting in a subset of new products to present to retailers.

The prior year's summit (not facilitated by our team) was initially deemed a success. People who participated in the summit were excited by the ideas that emerged from it, believing, at the time, that they had some real "winners" in their midst. However, in the months following the summit, as those ideas were further vetted and developed, this excitement waned.

More specifically, leaders of the organization felt that many of the ideas from the previous year lacked viability for the organization. They proved to be too niche (i.e., not big enough to capture the attention of Walmart) or too disconnected from the realities of the company's day-to-day operations and constraints. These reflections led my team and me to structure the work scope around the event differently than the prior year (engaging a mix of organizational leaders and end consumers throughout it).

Yet, we knew that this new structure alone wasn't going to be enough to circumvent the "value doubt" that was rampant in the minds of the senior leadership team. They deeply wanted this year's summit to be a success, but they were tired and anxious. Having little to show from last year's summit made the team doubtful. *Would the outcome be any different this year?*

They had tepidly agreed to sponsor the summit, but it was clear: The team needed more than a yes to the project to reignite hope for a different outcome. My team turned to the Treasure, Trash, Hope, Fear exercise to fuel a change in the perspective of the leaders engaged in this initiative.

Practically speaking, this meant displaying a two-by-two diagram, like the one illustrated.

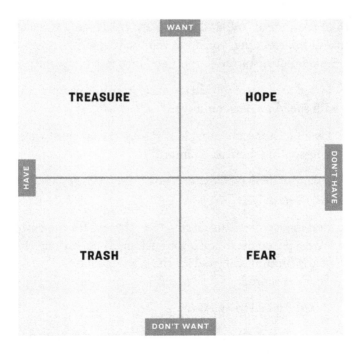

At project kickoff, we facilitated a conversation around that graphic.

I asked: "What did you 'Treasure' about last year's experience? What do you want to hold onto or further build upon this year?"

The team responded:

- "We have equity with our retailers today. We want to make sure that equity is protected."

- "We have a history of creating high-quality products that retailers value and rely on."

- "As an organization, we're willing to take risks when the conditions are right."

I then prompted: "What do you want to 'Trash' or discard? What didn't work that you don't want to repeat?"

Stakeholders started to relax and began to open up:

- "I want to let go of the red tape that prevents us from acting with speed on new initiatives."

- "I want to stop evaluating ideas based on our comfort level in presenting them to Walmart."

- "I want to drop the desire to be perfect. We get paralyzed with overanalysis."

We then moved on to discussing the "Hopes" for the current initiative. I posed the following question: "What do you 'Hope' this year's summit will yield for the organization?"

The team shared:

- "Greater speed to market."

- "A new sales model that helps us test and prove demand for new products."

- "A roadmap of the new product that we can produce, without worry of supply shortages."

And then, finally, I asked about the "Fears": "What 'Fears' or concerns do you have about stepping into this summit experience again?"

The stakeholders became vulnerable and shared:

- "I fear that our current brand can't stretch as far into the pet care category as we would like it to."

- "I fear that we will damage our retailer relationships if we miss the mark on these new pet care products."

- "I fear a loss of control if we use outside formulators in the creation of these new products."

The conversation was rich and heartfelt. The organization really wanted to expand into the broader pet care category, yet there were many roadblocks standing in the way of that happening—some self-designed and others not.

First, the company wanted to produce every product in their own factories. While this was a great aspiration, it hindered the broader reach that they said they wanted in the pet care industry—at least in the short term. The stakeholder team agreed that they would need to be open to challenging this cultural norm as we moved through the current summit experience, and in the further vetting and development work post-summit.

Second, the team wasn't confident that their current brand could transition easily into the broader pet care industry... or suspected it could stretch only so far. This meant company leaders hadn't yet decided whether to expand solely into nutrition-focused areas of pet care (thus staying aligned with their current brand) or to pursue new brands and partnerships to achieve the broader lifestyle positioning they envisioned. This lack of clarity led to a sense of paralysis in the team.

Additionally, the organization was suffering from major supply chain shortages because of COVID-19. The stress of that challenge was very real and in the forefront of decision-making at that moment.

Many of the stakeholders also talked about how the intent to innovate was a bit of an oxymoron in the organization. They talked about wanting to innovate and sponsored initiatives like the event we were in—the Innovation Summit. Yet, when it came to pulling the trigger on launching a new product into the market (particularly one for the broader pet care category), there was a lot of hesitation, risk aversion, red tape, etc. If we were going to go through this experience again, people wanted a tangible new product in the market as a result.

And, lastly, the organization was operating with the underlying assumption or belief that all the products they produced would need to be sold through Walmart to be deemed a success. Space on the Walmart shelf gives a manufacturer access to an extensive and diverse customer base, leading to increased visibility and brand recognition, sales volume, and competitive advantage. This client had a strong relationship with Walmart already but was fearful of losing it if they made the wrong growth moves in the category. They felt they needed a way to test these new products in the market—using online channels, for instance. However, at that time, they were at a loss for how to go about doing that.

As you can see, many fears and anxieties were bubbling under the surface for this team, emotions that, left unchecked, would have had the stakeholder team only half-heartedly engaging in the current summit experience. While we didn't fully address or resolve all the past *innovation baggage* of the team that day, we did bring that baggage into the light. That created the invitation among the team, throughout the initiative, to continue dialogues about the issues that had surfaced.

Fast-forward to today, this team has expanded their presence in the pet care industry and has created that "market testing" sales process that they spoke of back in this conversation. That process has helped to take the pressure off of immediate success; it's given them some space to walk before they have to run. Most importantly, they've achieved the goal that felt seemingly impossible at that moment: They now have an expanded portfolio of pet care products in the market.

I wholeheartedly believe that this thirty-minute conversation, and the summit that subsequently unfolded from there, was a catalytic force in supporting this company to be where it is today. I want you to support your stakeholders to have equally stimulating conversations and accelerated results. Let me tell you how.

Your Challenge:
Surface the Innovation Baggage

Your challenge is rather simple: Pump the brakes. Instead of plowing ahead, pretending that this initiative is the first time this type of project has been done, acknowledge that there's a past to consider. Some of this past might influence the current and future of your project, while some may not.

Your job, at this point, doesn't involve projecting or guessing what will impact your work. Rather, your job is about *getting it all out onto the table,* so that you can assess what *could* impact your work down the road. More specifically, there are *four types of innovation baggage* that I want you to address as you lead your team through an intentional dialogue about their previous, similar project experiences:

Your challenge
is rather simple:
Pump the brakes.

1   **Unresolved Issues:** Similar past projects might have triggered conflicts the organization never fully resolved. People might have swept those points of difference under the rug, but that doesn't mean they went away. They've just sat festering in the dark ... like the question from my story: *Can our brand really expand into the broader pet care category, beyond nutrition?* If these lingering issues stay hidden, they can strain communication and hinder collaboration within your stakeholder group.

2   **Emotional Burdens:** Your team may carry emotional baggage from past experiences, like resentment, mistrust, or insecurity. (In my case, the COVID-19 supply chain issues had triggered major feelings of insecurity in my stakeholders.) These emotional weights impact your work, innovator. Stakeholders might engage but withhold honest input or focus on setbacks—whether about the project or your leadership—while overlooking the progress achieved.

3   **Cultural Norms:** These refer to the team dynamics within your stakeholder group—power dynamics, communication styles, and decision-making processes. Understanding these is crucial, as they reveal which norms stakeholders are likely to challenge or accept. In my story, the organization had a cultural norm of only investing in products they could manufacture in-house. This norm, however, raised concerns about whether it would support the company's growth goals. Once this norm was made visible, the stakeholders collectively decided not to let it limit their thinking moving forward.

4   **Underlying Assumptions:** These are the internal narratives that people carry with them; the unspoken beliefs that dictate behaviors and decisions of a group. Going back to my

story, did my client really have to sell their product right out of the gate to Walmart in order to be a success? Apparently not. But at the start of the summit experience, they thought the answer to this question was yes.

I know, at this point, you might be saying, "Oh, Brianna, this sounds so negative. I don't want to dredge up the past like this. I want to start our project out with excitement and cheer. I just want to focus on moving forward and not looking backward."

I get that, but let me pose a slight reframe here: If you were guiding a group of teenagers on a ten-day backpacking trip and one of those individuals had a traumatic experience on a previous trip—say they got lost and spent a night by themselves in the freezing wilderness—you'd want to know this, right? It might make them timid and more worried. If you didn't know this, you'd be annoyed the entire time when this kid was asking a million questions and wouldn't wander further than two feet from you.

When you allow the team to speak of their past experiences—the good and the bad—you're setting yourself up as their capable, knowledgeable, and trustworthy *guide*.

Accept the Challenge: Facilitate the Treasure, Trash, Hope, Fear Exercise

The first thing you need to do is make the two-by-two diagram visible to the group you're engaging in dialogue with (look back at the illustration to support you in this).

I recommend that you draw this diagram on a whiteboard or use four big Post-it note pads, displayed in a grid. You can also easily facilitate this conversation in person or virtually. The medium and mode are not important. Having enough space to take notes in the quadrants is.

Start the dialogue with the "Treasure" quadrant. Ask: "In the past projects or initiatives, like the one we are about to embark on, what has worked well?" "What do we want to 'Treasure?'" "What do you want to continue?" Let the team talk and capture the highlights of the conversation as they do.

Once the dialogue around "Treasure" peters out, move to the "Trash" section and ask: "What do you hope to let go of or 'Trash?'" "What do you have but don't really want, as it's proven to be a disservice to you and the team in the past?"

Once that conversation comes to an end, move to the "Hope" quadrant and ask: "What are you really 'Hoping' the outcome of this work will be?" "What do you really want, but don't currently have?"

And, lastly, once the "Hope" dialogue has ceased, move to the "Fear" quadrant and ask: "What 'Fears' or concerns do you have about the project we're kicking off?" "What do you *not* want to have happen in this project or as a result of it?"

As the conversation unfolds, listen for the *unresolved issues, emotional burdens, cultural norms,* and *underlying assumptions* that seem to dictate the way things have always been done for this team. Stay curious and ask probing questions to dig deeper.

Structuring the conversation into these four discussion quadrants—"Treasure," "Trash," "Hope," and "Fear"—allows your stakeholders to have a potentially vulnerable conversation about what they truly desire for the project without unnecessary discomfort, tension, and insecurity.

What to Expect

When you lean into this Treasure, Trash, Hope, Fear exercise, you give your stakeholders the space to take full stock of where they are. You permit them to put voice to how their past experiences inform their current realities. The result is that they feel seen and heard and thus, more connected and empowered as a team. They feel that you, as their leader, really know their challenges and that you're working *with them* to ensure positive outcomes of their current initiative.

They also often feel a sense of relief. Through this dialogue, you've given them an outlet to speak about the fears and anxieties they have about their project. The simple act of putting voice to those worries instantly disarms them. No longer does each stakeholder feel as though they're carrying the weight of these worries by themselves. The whole team can now work in partnership to mitigate them.

And on top of that, you now know what roadblocks might stand in the way of the current project's success. You also have awareness of where you might lean in throughout the initiative to help the team settle some of their unresolved issues or cleanse some of their emotional burdens. You have insight into some of the cultural norms or underlying assumptions that you might need to challenge to support the team in meeting their goals.

It's crucial to recognize that it's not your responsibility or within your authority to resolve all the unresolved issues or emotional burdens your team may carry. Nor is it your role to fix the cultural norms or implicit beliefs that could hinder progress. However, you can serve as their guide, supporting them in reaching greater heights than they've ever reached before.

Mindset Shift: Surface the Innovation Baggage

When your project resembles one that the organization has tackled in the past, pump the brakes. Use the Treasure, Trash, Hope, Fear exercise to support the processing of past *innovation baggage*—the unresolved issues, emotional burdens, cultural norms, and underlying assumptions that might impact your current work together. You'll be rewarded with a more connected, empowered, and engaged team.

7

Define Your Core
Leadership Values

NEWER INNOVATION LEADERS frequently make the mistake of prioritizing the needs and well-being of their team above their own. The belief underpinning this leadership approach is that selfless leaders are loved leaders. I have personally traveled the road of selfless leadership, and I'm here to tell you that this is false. I often refer to those days in my company as the "dark days of Sylver Consulting," days that ended in burnout, resentment, and a toxic work culture.

At that time, I was putting everyone else's needs before my own. This looked like

- consistently working late nights and weekends, believing that I needed to always be available to support my team and my clients—or else (though I couldn't even articulate what the "or else" was at the time);

- taking on unmanageable workloads, trying to shield my team from being overburdened;

- ignoring my own health—skipping meals, neglecting exercise, sacrificing sleep—all in service to my team and my clients;

- failing to delegate tasks that could easily be shared with others, again for fear of overburdening my team;

- absorbing team conflicts and personally mediating bouts of emotional and mental stress so that others could feel comfortable again as quickly as possible.

I thought I was being of service to others in a constructive and positive way at that time. But I wasn't. Far from it! My allegiance to selfless leadership led to feelings of resentment and burnout for me. On top of that, I wasn't leveraging my team effectively and there was an obvious undercurrent of toxicity within it. The people working for me at that time weren't growing at the pace that they should in their roles because I was trying too hard to be the martyr who was "protecting" them from having too much on their plate. We weren't walking in lockstep with one another. We were all focused on what everyone *wasn't doing* or the skills they *didn't have*, and the competition within the team, at times, was destructive. It was a lonely era for me as a leader and not a time I look back on with pride.

That said, I extend grace to myself, as I know I needed to go through all of that. I needed to experience the pain and suffering of that moment to grow to where I am today—a servant leader—operating a highly effective team that respects one another and operates productively and systematically towards three core values: shared appreciation, collaboration, and personal responsibility.

It took me hitting rock bottom, in those "dark days," to get to this point. I had to define the core values of my organization to capture the light that fuels and guides us in everything that we do. I'm hoping, dear innovator, that this chapter and the challenge within it helps you to skip the "rock bottom" part, so that you and your teams can get to the thriving part of your story much quicker.

What It Looks Like

First, I needed to acknowledge that I was a mess. I'm a recovering perfectionist, meaning my mode of operation—at that time—was to do everything myself because then I could control how it got done. This worked fine from an effectiveness perspective, when I was a solo entrepreneur. But as my team grew and our book of business grew, these perfectionist tendencies weren't helpful. In fact, they were crippling.

At the time, one scene ran in my head on repeat: I was dragging my team up a mountain toward victory, trying to capture the flag at the peak. When we got to the peak, I was so emotionally depleted that I no longer cared about the victory. In that season of my business, almost *every* project depleted me. And nearly weekly, I needed a full veg-out evening just to cope. No bueno!

As I reflect on that time, I can see so clearly what this imagery was telling me. It was God's nudge to say, "Brianna, you are overwhelmed and burdened by your responsibility as the leader of this team. You are working for your team rather than them working for you. You're not experiencing joy in this relentless struggle for achievement. You need to delegate more. You need to reflect on your team's dynamics. And you need to consider *how* you're leading. It's time to make changes."

When I got to that rock-bottom moment, I turned to my journal for help processing all that I was going through. I had what looked like a thriving business from the outside, but under the surface, it was a trainwreck. In my journal, I wrote down everything I hated about what was happening, everything that caused me sadness and insecurity as a leader. I didn't filter what went on the page; anything was game—no matter how mean and childish it was, I captured it all.

I wrote about the us-versus-them mentality that was fueling so much of the negativity, anger, and judgment in my team. I wrote about the overemphasis on "not enough," how I felt like our team was seeing only what we (the leadership of Sylver and the broader team) *weren't* doing, rather than looking for the good. I also wrote about how people weren't following through and doing what they said they were going to do, how this was putting a strain on our client relationships and project timelines.

When I felt like I had exhausted all the negative tensions in my heart, I wrote down everything I did value about how the team was operating. Our best moments were when we came together for project sensemaking, when we met to articulate strategic implications of project insights. I was proud of our project output and the growth being unlocked for our clients as a result. I was also excited for the niche that our company was carving out in the industry, sitting at the intersection of three disciplines: user experience, market research, and strategy. Clients were taking notice of how this unique combination of skills enabled innovation in a more holistic and integrated way, and demand for our services was growing.

At the end of that journaling session, I had a messy list of the good, the bad, and the ugly. When I pulled back and studied it all—the positive and the negative—I realized that there were patterns. All the things I had written down pointed to the three values that now orient everything we do at Sylver Consulting: shared appreciation, collaboration, and personal responsibility. Defining these values, of course, was not the answer, in and of itself. It was just the beginning.

Now, with these values defined, I needed to align the team on how to bring these values to life on a day-to-day basis. I knew this next step wasn't going to happen overnight. Getting the team to live and breathe these core values was going to take consistent effort over an extended period of time. It would also require ongoing, careful reflection to ensure that the interventions being tested were delivering the desired outcomes.

It took a while for these truths to set in and even more time to develop new core practices and rhythms as a leader to change my reality. But I was persistent, and I sought support for myself. This was the moment in my career when I started to invest in leadership training (something that I continue to do to this day).

Now, many years on the other side of this moment, there's a new scene that runs in my head: I see a circle of people all holding parts of a parachute. I see the joy on the faces of everyone in that circle as we work together to catch the wind with that parachute. And as we trap ourselves in that parachute's wind, I see us rolling on the ground in laughter, just like toddlers often do in a mommy and me music class.

This scene embodies the carefree joy that characterizes my team today:

- We lead in appreciation of everyone's efforts and strengths—and how those come together to support our shared success.

- We embrace a collaborative spirit in everything we do, creating a sense of unity and teamwork that's truly magical.

- We follow through—without fail—on our responsibilities. No one needs to check up on each other; we simply trust that everyone will deliver.

I'm proud of the culture that we nurture at Sylver Consulting. Getting here has taken a lot of work, but I was committed to the long haul when the need for change was presented to me. And those efforts have paid off. Today, we use these core values not only to orient our work, but also to guide our hiring and firing practices. These values represent the core essence of our team, and when people are aligned in action and mindset towards these values, they thrive. When they don't, friction exists, and their tenure is often stunted. These values have radically changed me as a leader, and I hope and pray the same will be true for you.

Your Challenge: Turn the Mirror Inward

I've put this chapter into "Suiting Up" because establishing rhythms that reinforce your core values as a leader is critical to your team's success. However, you first must create those values, which is not a trivial task!

Defining your leadership values is a *heart* task, not a *head* task—meaning I want you to develop your leadership values based on your own personal passions, emotions, and values, not through logic and analytical thinking. This is going to require you to be vulnerable with yourself. You must be willing to turn the mirror inward and critically look at yourself and your team—zeroing in on what's working and where you might be falling short today. At times, you might not like what you see. However, the more honest you are with yourself, the stronger your core leadership values will be.

And strong values are catalytic. The best ones have the power to shape your teams and the people within them, not just describe who you are. To that end, once your values are defined, lead with them as if they are the foundation

Defining your leadership values *is a **heart** task, not a **head** task.*

of everything you do, as if everything depends on it. Why? Because it does!

Strong values attract the right people and weed out the wrong people from your team. They help to bring alignment to the actions of a team, making the path to greatness more friction-free and fun. And people love and want to be a part of a team with clear direction and values. They foster engagement and purpose at work.

Remember, teams don't change—people do. And when people change, your team evolves.

If you want to shift your team's culture, it starts by changing the mindsets of its members—and that begins with you!

Accept the Challenge: Create and Activate Your Leadership Values

Taking time to define your leadership values is good at any time, regardless of whether you've got your own rock-bottom moment happening or just want to enable more overall team effectiveness. To do this exercise effectively, you'll need a journal. (And yes, it's important that you put *pen* to *paper* when doing this. The physical act of writing channels energy differently than when using a computer; for instance, it engages your brain more and allows you to remember things better and make connections more easily.)

This is a three-part exercise that you should commit to doing over multiple days or weeks.

Part 1: Journal on past team and leadership experiences
You're going to write responses to four questions:

1   What's not working about my team or what hasn't worked about teams I've led in the past?

2 What's not working about my leadership? Where am I failing myself or my team today? How have I failed myself or my teams in the past?

3 What *is* working about my team or has worked well in teams I've led in the past?

4 What *is* working about my leadership today or how I've led teams in the past?

As you engage in this writing activity, keep these guidelines front and center:

- Be specific and exhaustive in your responses to these questions.

- Avoid bullet-point answers.

- Don't filter your thoughts and feelings. Allow yourself to be mean or childish, if you need to. (If you're worried about anyone seeing what you've written after the fact, commit to tearing or burning it up. Just don't censor what you choose to put on the paper).

Part 2: Identify patterns

Once you've exhausted all the details that you can in response to these four questions, read over your notes. As you do, look for concepts or phrases that repeatedly show up in your text. Also, highlight other phrases that stand out to you as important. And then transfer all those highlighted phrases onto sticky notes. You'll want each phrase to have its own sticky note.

With sticky notes now in hand, cluster similar phrases together. Then look for a word or phrase that best describes that collection of sticky notes in the aggregate. Title the cluster of sticky notes with that word or phrase.

From my journaling activity, for instance, I had a series of phrases that I ultimately described as "shared appreciation"—the value of knowing and appreciating each other as people. This value for me embodied the desire for mutual recognition, gratitude, and respect within the team. Some of the phrases that patterned together to create this value were the following:

From my What's Not Working about My Team list:

- My team doesn't know or appreciate one another as people, outside of the job they perform at Sylver.

- I have team members in my office every week complaining about one another, yet they aren't trying to address those concerns with one another directly.

From my What's Not Working about My Leadership list:

- I feel like I'm working for my employees—giving a lot and gaining very little in return. I'm questioning whether I want to own a company that has employees.

- Employees have a Slack channel dedicated to lamenting about how terrible my leadership is.

From my What *Is* Working about My Team list:

- We thrive as a team when we come together to sense-make around insights or to translate those insights into next-step actions on behalf of a client.

- I feel like the team believes in the work we're doing and the impacts we're enabling.

From my What *Is* Working about My Leadership list:

- I'm actively and intentionally extending grace to others on the team and myself.

- I've now got awareness of my perfectionist tendencies (thanks to my business mentor) and the negative impacts they are having on the emotional well-being of myself and my team. Awareness is the first step of change, right?

Part 3: Define consistent actions
that will breathe life into those values

Go back to each of those patterned phrases and ask yourself: *What consistent actions can I or the team do to bring this value to life?*

In my scenario, we immediately embraced two actions to mobilize the value of "shared appreciation," both of which we still practice today. We added two segments of conversation into our Monday morning team meeting. Responding to the insight that our team didn't know one another as people, we now start each Monday by having everyone share how they're feeling coming into the week. Team members often share highlights and low points that happened to them over the weekend, and they communicate the energy that they're bringing into the week ahead. We also, in that same meeting, give appreciation shout-outs to team members who went above and beyond the week before. Everyone contributes, counteracting the tendencies of people to look for the bad instead of the good or to be overly critical of one another instead of supportive.

These small additions to the Monday morning team meeting made an immediate impact on the connectedness of our team. Over time, I've seen how these interactions have changed team culture. No longer do people orient with a hint of skepticism, question motives, or talk behind people's backs. Rather, the assumption of positive intent is omnipresent within our team and people actively dialogue with one another about conflicts, when and if they arise.

"Patience" is the guiding virtue of this challenge, innovator.

Taking the time to define my leadership values was pivotal to my growth as a leader—a gift that I pray and hope you'll seize for yourself. The increased clarity and direction I gained regarding my own priorities has led to improved alignment and focus for my team. They know what I value and, therefore, they prioritize the actions that support shared appreciation, collaboration, and personal responsibility. That clarity has led to a stronger, more cohesive team. Work is much more fun these days, and our clients benefit from having engaged, accountable, and adaptable team members serving them on a day-to-day basis.

What to Expect

"Patience" is the guiding virtue of this challenge, innovator. Sitting down to define your core values can be a daunting task. Instead of feeling pressured to do it all in one sitting, I encourage you to allow the activity to occur over a period of time.

Break this task into multiple chunks. On Day 1, for instance, take one or two hours to do Part 1 of the exercise. Journal about the four questions on your team and leadership. Then on Day 2, come back to what you've written and do the Part 2 work of identifying patterns, clustering those patterns, and then finally naming them. Over the course of multiple days or weeks, you can then brainstorm actions for how to institutionalize those values in the teams you lead. Try some of the actions and track what your experience is like.

Most of your team will respond well to the positive changes. Expect renewed energy, excitement, and a sense of momentum. As people feel more comfortable sharing ideas without judgment, you'll begin to see stronger relationships, communication, and collaboration within the team.

However, some may resist the changes, feeling uneasy with the new levels of accountability and performance expectations. Offer these individuals grace and time to adapt. But if they continue to resist, you may need to reconsider their fit on the team, as unchecked negativity can undermine the positive culture you're building.

Hopefully, like me, you'll gain some early wins, giving you confidence that you're on the right track. However, know that it will take time to see and reap the full rewards of increased team cohesion and high performance.

You're playing a long game here, innovator. You can't just put words on a wall and call it good. You have to systematize these values throughout your work—intentionally, over time, day in and day out. You can't do it all at once. I recommend that you choose a few things, commit to them, and evaluate how they're working. As needed, pivot. And continue to add tactics, as seems appropriate.

Mindset Shift: Turn the Mirror Inward

Examine your team and leadership experiences to identify patterns. Use these patterns to create core leadership values that speak to your passions and priorities. Then look for ways to breathe life into those values day in and day out—for yourself and for your team. Doing so will change you and the people you work with, resulting in a stronger, more coherent team.

PART TWO

Free

Fall

"To be fully alive, fully human, and completely awake is to be continually thrown out of the nest."

PEMA CHÖDRÖN

THE PREVIOUS CHAPTERS have included all the things that you can *plan for* as an innovator: activities or steps that you can and should take, consistently and repeatedly, to set yourself—and the teams that you're leading—up for success. In essence, all the things we discussed in the last set of chapters are challenges you have some power to control. They're about packing your parachute and setting your flight path. They're about readying yourself for a successful jump into innovation.

In contrast, this next set of chapters is about the opposite: circumstances that might arise during an innovation initiative, seemingly out of nowhere. These aren't situations that you can plan for. They aren't situations you can control. Rather, these are situations you need to *deal with* in *real time*.

In many ways, these circumstances can leave you questioning why you're doing what you're doing and if you're the right person to be doing it. These are the moments in your work when things get difficult. In the face of that adversity, it's not uncommon to want to quit, complain really loudly, or shut down altogether.

Much like the free fall of skydiving, you'll feel like you're falling through the sky in these moments—disoriented, untethered, and possibly overwhelmed. This next set of chapters is about helping you gain perspective in these more challenging times of project free fall, or what I call the *messy middle of innovation*.

I'm a firm believer that nothing happens *to* you, but rather *for* you. Hence, the tools, activities, and reflections in the chapters to come will support you, dear innovator, to use these *yikes!* free fall moments as opportunities to access new levels of growth and expansion, both for yourself and for all those you're leading. To that end, my prayer is that you'll use this section of the book as an ongoing resource: that it becomes a playbook for you, a guide that you repeatedly turn to for advice as you're experiencing bouts of anxiety, defeat, or concern in your work.

Are you ready to jump? I've got you. Let's do this...

8

Tame the Skeptics

A N IDEAL INNOVATION TEAM is one that's fully energized—
brimming with creativity, curiosity, and excitement.
They're driven by collaboration, they're focused on making an impact, and they're enjoying the process along
the way.

You might call this kind of team *The Dream Team*. And it *is* a
dream because, unfortunately, it's not usually the reality. Lots
of emotions—particularly skepticism—can get in the way of the
ease and flow that supports and sustains this vibe we all crave.

When you find yourself in this situation—where skepticism
reigns—you can spend a lot of time feeling irritated or frustrated. Or you can *choose* to see the skepticism as a roadblock
to actively acknowledge and overcome. In this chapter, I'm
challenging you to tackle the skepticism *head-on*.

The first thing you need to know is that there's a scale of
skepticism, ranging from slight to strong, and your antidote
differs depending on the intensity of the doubt. The challenge
of this chapter is to first diagnose the level of skepticism that
you're experiencing and then to have the gumption to lean
in and shine a light on it. Doing so will protect the forward
momentum of your project.

What It Looks Like

I was working with a new client, a healthcare device manufacturer, who had recently launched an upgrade to their product. It wasn't a "next generation" product release (meaning it didn't have a ton of new features or capabilities embedded in it) but the organization had redesigned it to make their clinician users' workflows smoother and less burdensome. The team was really excited about this product update; they felt it was a huge improvement. Yet, when they released the product, the market's reaction told a contrasting story. In fact, many customers reached out to the company and requested to cancel their contracts. Something was obviously amiss.

They brought in my team at Sylver Consulting to help clarify their clients' definition of "customer success," so they could determine which improvements might best quiet the calls for canceled contracts and appease upset clients.

Our first step involved planning a two-day workshop with about two dozen people from across the organization, each representing different functional areas and different touch points associated with the product's design and delivery (from the product team themselves to customer service to training and implementation to sales, and many more). Our goal, during this session, was to download everything the team knew about "customer success" today so that we could use this information for further discussion and co-creation with their clients.

Everything was moving along well, and my team and the organization's leaders were excited to get to the bottom of the misalignment. That is, until the afternoon before the mandatory workshop, when a third of the attendees decided, en masse, to decline the meeting. Yes—this was a premeditated act of rebellion by a big portion of the workforce, championed by one member of the broader stakeholder team who was not interested in "wasting their time" in a two-day workshop. This act of rebellion caused a flurry of concern and worry among the project's core planning team. We needed *all the people* on the meeting invite to attend to make this session worthwhile, but it was clear that not everyone wanted to be there.

After some discussion, the president of the organization decided to throw the gauntlet down. He sent out a communication to the workforce reminding them that this workshop was a *mandatory meeting* and that there would be consequences if they didn't show up—both in physical presence at the meeting and emotional investment in the conversation once there.

What a great way to meet the broader stakeholder team of a brand-new client, right?! At least a third of the participants didn't want to be there and now they've just been told by their leader, "You will be there or else . . ."

As the lead facilitator of this now very charged meeting (tough market position and rebellious internal dynamic), I had a choice to make. I could proceed with the meeting 100 percent as planned. Or I could start the meeting acknowledging the events of the past twenty-four hours. It was bold (and I'm not going to lie—I, and the other core leads of the project, were shaking in our boots a bit), but we decided to start the meeting recognizing that a significant portion of the people in that room didn't want to be there.

As team members walked into the workshop, I could feel the tension. The negative energy was palpable. Once everyone was seated and settled, I didn't waste a beat. I briefly introduced myself and proceeded to address the elephant in the room:

I know a lot of you don't want to be here and are wondering who I am. I'm not a nurse. I don't have technical expertise around your product. I know you don't have two days to spare and that you're working around-the-clock to deliver the services you currently provide to clients. You're fearful that this workshop will be a waste of your time and will not really help the organization get to a better place in the market.

Before we jump into our work for the next two days, I want to discuss why you don't want to be here ... or at least what makes you uncomfortable or concerned about being here. This is going to be a discussion that *everyone* participates in. The goal is to get all the dark, festering thoughts out in the open and onto the wall. Once you all have expressed those concerns and thoughts, we'll go through them one by one and I'll tell you how and where in our project we'll address each one. For any concerns that the project can't specifically address, Ted (the president) will respond to them.

I gave everyone a few minutes to collect their thoughts. Each person had a pen and paper at their seat. Then, we started the discussion. I went around the room and, one by one, asked every participant in the room, "What's making you concerned or uncomfortable about being here today?" As each person spoke, I jotted down their response on big Post-it notes stuck to the wall of the conference room. After each person shared their perspective, I looked them in the eyes and said, "Thank you." Then, I moved on to the next person in the room. I went around the room and asked that same question again—three times to each person, with no change to the question prompt. I jotted down more notes, said more thank-yous, and by the end of the conversation, we had a clear list of why many didn't want to be there that day.

I had a team of moderate and strong skeptics that I was leading—oh boy! Some of the skepticism stemmed from the participants' past experiences (i.e., gathering to discuss and plan for initiatives that never got off the ground or never gained traction). Yet, a lot of the skepticism wasn't really about the work we were there to do, but more about how stretched the team was feeling at work at that moment.

The organization was rapidly scaling in the market, but their delivery systems weren't yet optimized to work at that level. Therefore, everyone was working around-the-clock and feared that this initiative would just add more to their plates, which were already maxed. They felt like they didn't have the time to be in the room, and they definitely didn't think they had the capacity to take on any new tasks that might come from the work session. This was all great context for me and the core team.

After everyone had voiced their concerns, I went through each item on the list. Most of the issues raised would be addressed by the current project design. Our goal wasn't to pile more on their plates, but to streamline their efforts to better align with what their customers saw as "success." A few concerns needed ongoing attention throughout the initiative, while others were matters the president would need to handle personally.

This whole dialogue took about sixty minutes, so it definitely ate into our workshop agenda in a big way. However, there was a tangible energy shift in the room after the conversation. We didn't miraculously have an unskeptical team. But we had moved this team—in an hour—from a position of moderate and strong skepticism to a position of slight skepticism. *I'll take it*, I thought. *I can work with the pushback of slight skepticism and still make traction on this project.*

And traction was gained. We learned, through the project, that my client was taking on more responsibility than was needed in delivering "customer success." We also confirmed that the market pushback was not *really* related to the product,

By definition, innovation takes people **out of their comfort zone.**

but rather to the systems around the product, like training and implementation and customer service. The delivery model needed to be streamlined, which actually meant *less work* on the plates of the key stakeholders once the new systems had been put in place. The result was more manageable workflows for the skeptics and happier clients, overall.

I also take a bit of pride in the fact that the person who sparked the mass declining of my workshop invite at the start of the initiative came up to me at the end of it, expressing how grateful she was to have had my team's support. She actually asked to give me a hug of appreciation, which I gratefully accepted!

Your Challenge: Get to the Root of Skepticism

As an innovation leader, the skepticism you encounter will vary in intensity. That level of intensity will guide how you should address and shed light on the doubts that could hinder your project.

Slight skeptics will harbor mild doubts or reservations about your project but will still be open to the process and the potential outcomes. The best thing you can do when leading a *slightly* skeptical team is to keep moving. Give people space to share their concerns as much as possible (in the context of the work) and offer past stories and case studies as ways to alleviate their concerns. Largely speaking, however, this team needs to live the process of innovation to emerge as believers and advocates for it. It's OK if they're not 100 percent comfortable every step of the way. By definition, innovation takes people out of their comfort zone. Therefore, a certain level of skepticism is to be expected.

Moderate skeptics will question the validity or feasibility of your project and its outcomes yet will still be willing to show up and be engaged (even if begrudgingly, at times). When dealing with *moderately* skeptical teams, you'll likely feel resistance in an acute way. Some even describe this resistance as "leading through quicksand," meaning you feel like you're expending a lot of energy to make progress, with little to show from that effort. In these instances, it's advantageous for you to pause your work and bring the root of the skepticism into the light. Continuing to push through and avoiding the palpable resistance will only sink your team further into the quicksand. Not to mention, the outcomes of your work will suffer.

Strong skeptics will focus on issues that are no longer about the project, or the innovation process itself. In these cases, comments often center around a distrust of leadership, specifically the leadership's ability to act on the outcomes of the work (and the fear that people are just wasting their time). When you're dealing with a *strongly* skeptical team, it's not uncommon for people to quit showing up to participate in the work. If they do show up in body, they're often not there in spirit. In these instances, much like when you're dealing with a moderately skeptical team, it's important to pause the work and talk about the root of the skepticism. You'll find that, in these moments, your team members often need reassurance—*by leadership*—that the energy and effort they're pouring into this work is important and valued.

When dealing with *moderately* or *strongly* skeptical teams, it's important to create the space for candid conversation about everyone's concerns. It's also important to do this in a group setting, as a way to hold everyone accountable for the concerns and feelings they choose to express. This means that you (and other sponsors or leaders of the work) need to be open to facilitating a difficult and potentially negative dialogue (at least in the beginning). You'll also need to endure the discomfort of not knowing fully how that conversation will go down or what will come out of it.

From an innovator's perspective, this is a tough and stressful conversation to facilitate. But I assure you that when you choose to bravely and courageously embrace it, you'll supercharge the success potential of your team. Let me show you how.

Accept the Challenge: Facilitate a Group Loop Activity

If you're coming face-to-face with skepticism that's preventing forward momentum on a project, I encourage you to make the space for a Group Loop activity. Claim the sixty minutes or so required to empower your team to put voice to the skepticism that's immobilizing them, so that you can discern how best to address the root cause of the skepticism and define how to move forward.

The step-by-step process for facilitating the Group Loop activity is simple:

1   Before you begin this exercise, decide on your centering and repeating question for the group. The question will be unique to your project and the context that has brought you to the Group Loop moment. In the case of my story, the centering question was, "What's making you concerned or uncomfortable about being here today?" You can also be blunter and ask, "Why do you feel this project is likely to fail?" Or, "Why do you feel this initiative is a 'waste of time'?"

2   When you get in front of your skeptical team, openly address the elephant in the room. What you choose to share here should be based on facts (i.e., one third of the attendees in this room declined to come to this meeting yesterday)

or things you've heard (i.e., team members doubt my competency to lead this initiative, given my lack of training as a nurse or lack of technical expertise in the product domain). Be *very careful* of your tone, avoiding any tinge of defensiveness. Instead, be more matter-of-fact without conveying any sense of judgment.

3 Set expectations for how the activity will work. Share the question you want each person to respond to and tell them that you'll ask each person to share three responses to this question, in a round-robin fashion. For you, as the facilitator of this conversation, know that the round-robin solicitation of responses is important. With each share, every person's answers will get deeper and more refined, particularly as they take in and process, in real time, the broader team's feelings and opinions.

4 Once the setup is complete, ask each participant to share their response, out loud, in three to five words. Assure them that you're not judging their answers and that you'll be writing down key points to circle back to later. After each person's share, simply say, "Thank you." Don't respond to the point; don't ask for clarity; just record their responses in a way that's visible to the broader group.

5 Once everyone has answered the question multiple times (three times per person is ideal), go back and address each key point, one by one. Explain how your project plan will address the concerns shared. If the current plan doesn't address the concern, but could be adjusted to address it, voice what those adjustments could be. And acknowledge, openly and honestly, which concerns are out of scope for the current project.

What to Expect

Let's first just acknowledge how vulnerable you're going to feel shining a light on the skepticism that's plaguing your team. If there was ever a moment in your work where things could go sideways, where the situation could get worse before it gets better, this is it. I share this not to scare you, but because I want you to know that *I know* that what I'm asking of you is not an easy task. However, it is essential, as it's a proven technique for paving the way for more productive and impactful innovation work.

This Group Loop activity is never part of your original project roadmap. It's a detour that you're forced to take (and will likely try to avoid). Believe me, you'll be tempted to try to plow through the skepticism hoping that, with time, people will simply get on board.

If you're dealing with a slightly skeptical team, that tactic of avoidance can work and is the preferred path forward, in fact. For the moderately or strongly skeptical teams, however, that avoidance behavior will only come back to bite you in the butt.

I urge you, innovator, to address the skepticism head-on. Once you've made the root of the team's skepticism visible, respond to those concerns with care and respect. Demonstrate, through your commentary, that you understand their reservations and that you're committed to either addressing those concerns in the context of your work or working with others in the organization—as best you can—to address them.

It's important to understand that this activity is unlikely to turn a skeptical team into *The Dream Team*. Rather, the goal is to ratchet down the skepticism, to downgrade a *moderately* or *strongly* skeptical team to a *slightly* skeptical team. They don't need to fully trust or believe in the innovation process after this Group Loop activity; they just need to be willing to take the next step in it, trusting that you've got them in that process.

After an activity like this, it's crucial to remember that your team is watching closely. They're gauging whether you'll follow through on your promises, address their concerns, and meet the timelines you set. It's vital to deliver on what you've committed to, as every action you take shows the team that you've listened and value their input. This consistent follow-through helps reduce doubt and insecurity, creating a more confident and assured team.

If, for some reason, you can't meet an expectation, be transparent, address it honestly with the group, and explain why. Consistency in how you lead is how you'll keep your team walking in faith with you. And hopefully, in time, they do become firm believers—and even advocates—for your work and your process... just likely not today!

Mindset Shift: Get to the Root of Skepticism

When you find yourself leading a team crippled by skepticism, create the space to candidly address the elephants in the room. Use the Group Loop activity to uncover the concerns holding your team back. Your goal isn't to turn skeptics into full believers, but to shift strong or moderate skeptics into slight ones. A slightly skeptical team will still walk with you, trusting the process even if they don't fully understand every part of what you're asking... just yet.

9

Own Your Strengths

PICTURE YOURSELF in this scenario: You're meeting with a group of people who have been called together to address a specific topic of importance. The organizers of this meeting have intentionally gathered a variety of technical experts on the topic. Each person's viewpoint is crucial to crafting a new action path for the problem in discussion, and the pressure to address that issue is acute.

The meeting begins. As each person introduces themself, they share who they are, what their role and function in the organization is, why they're excited for this project, and what they specifically feel they bring to the table in the context of the topic at hand. And then it's your turn and you say something like this: "Hi. My name is Brianna Sylver. I'm here supporting this team as a process expert. I'm not a technical expert on this topic—nor will I pretend to be one. However, I am an expert on things like problem-solving, creativity, collaboration, and the rigor it takes to yield impactful outcomes on sticky problems like the one we're facing right now. I'm going to lead this team through an innovation process designed to create a portfolio of ideas that will support the organization to move through this challenge and thrive once on the other side."

What do you think the other technical experts in that room do? How do they react to you?

More times than not, they size you up and immediately dismiss you. Your perceived value as a meaningful contributor to the work sank a couple of percentage points as soon as you said that you had no technical expertise qualifying you to be in the room.

The truth is that people tend to value process expertise only after they've experienced it. The good news? You've been invited to be part of this initiative, which means *someone* in the room recognizes the value you bring to solving the current challenge. The downside? Not everyone at the table shares that belief yet, so it's now your job to demonstrate your worth to the rest of the team.

What It Looks Like

Sylver Consulting was hired to facilitate an autonomous shipping cohort. This cohort was established to address the logistics, regulations, and technology for fully autonomous cargo ships. Its members were AI and robotics developers, representing a variety of maritime and transportation authorities. The cohort involved ten entities and aimed to advance and sustain efforts to develop autonomous navigation systems that meet maritime safety and operational standards.

The talent on the cohort planning team was intentional: Two technical experts, plus me, would meet monthly to design each cohort connection. The two technical experts knew everything there was to know about maritime safety and operational standards. I knew how to design impactful and effective meetings.

As we started working together, I was up-front about not having technical expertise in maritime safety and operational standards. And that fact made it really hard for my counter-parts to trust me, initially. After all, my role was to design cohort meetings that encouraged reflection, collaboration, and swift action toward developing autonomous navigation systems that meet maritime safety standards. However, from their perspective, I didn't seem to have the abilities to perform that role, nor did I have a track record of facilitating cohorts around this topic.

Bottom line: They questioned my purpose on the team (and the sanity of the organization that hired me to lead this group). I was in a position of needing to build trust with my team-mates—trust that I knew was not going to be won overnight.

For the first three meetings, the technical experts ran the show—marginalizing me in the process. They structured these meetings lecture-style, where a presenter spoke—for nearly the entire hour—on a topic appropriate for the cohort. (There were perhaps five to ten minutes left for questions at the end of the hour.) This meeting format limited dialogue and reflection, hindering progress toward the cohort's goal of leveraging the power of the group to collectively advance autonomous navi-gation systems that meet maritime safety standards.

During each cohort planning meeting, I respectfully suggested ways to structure the conversation to encourage re-flection and commitment to next steps. Yet, my ideas were consistently dismissed. I wasn't influencing the design of these cohort sessions; instead, I was stuck in an administrative role. I was growing restless.

There was no question that my value as a process expert—for this cohort—was not being realized. I decided that a difficult conversation with the planning team was needed.

I started the conversation in this way: "It's become clear that my lack of technical expertise in this domain is preventing us from collaborating in an effective way toward the design and execution of this cohort. My value, as a process expert, is going unrealized in how these cohort connections are being facilitated. I believe it's best for me to step away from this project and that the funds for my consulting hours be redirected to something more impactful for the cohort."

The lead technical expert was visibly frustrated. "You can't leave this project, Brianna. We don't have the bandwidth to do this if you're not helping with the logistics."

"OK," I replied. "But I can't keep acting as only the cohort's secretary. You aren't leveraging my expertise. I'm not a technical expert and I won't pretend to be. But what I am gifted at is crafting communication that drives people to understand, interpret, and take action. The purpose of this cohort is to accelerate action through collaboration. That's what I do for a living. It's what I've built an entire consultancy around. So, if you want me to stay in this cohort, I need permission to run the next meeting as a collaborative, co-creative engagement. Afterward, we can assess together if what transpires is in alignment with your long-term vision for the cohort. I sense it will be."

The lead technical expert was visibly torn. She needed my work hours to logistically support the cohort's execution, but she had no confidence that I had the chops to craft and lead the cohort's discussion around maritime safety and operational standards. After some cautious consideration, however, she said, "OK."

I designed the upcoming meeting using a Communities of Practice format, with a lot of intentional space set aside for productive, sensemaking conversation.

Going into that conversation, my technical experts were nervous. Every second of the agenda was not packed with content. In fact, the space in the agenda was sparking a tremendous amount of anxiety for my teammates prior to the meeting: "What if no one says anything?" "What if we have someone go off on a tangent?" "What if we have one person dominate the conversation?" "What if no one steps forward to share?" I tried to assuage their fears: "I am a facilitator of conversation. This is what I am gifted at. Let me do this. I've got this." They tepidly gave me the floor.

That next one-hour cohort meeting went beautifully! For the first time since the cohort started, we had an *engaged* group. Twenty-three people, from across the ten participating entities, showed up to that connection—the highest turnout of any cohort meeting up to that point. And the majority of the cohort participated in that connection not just by audio but on video— yet another marker of engagement. We had been asking people to join via video for the previous two cohort connections, but the majority of people did not, which I hypothesized meant they were multitasking—doing another task, while the cohort presentation was on "in the background." In this meeting, the conversation of the cohort was in the foreground of their attention, which was a very good thing, especially towards its goal of advancing autonomous navigation systems that meet maritime safety standards.

The conversation of that cohort connection was both *productive and inspirational*; cohort members defined it as "part therapy, part content." Every person felt seen and heard, like they were no longer alone, working on their autonomous navigation system strategies on an island, isolated. They felt like they were now part of a group, like they were supported in their work in a new way. Each person walked away from that time ready to take next-step actions—that were implemented as early as *that* day—in support of fueling forward momentum in their work. That meeting was a slam-dunk success.

And that success was acknowledged by the lead technical expert. When that meeting wrapped up, she turned to me and said, "Wow, Brianna, you really do know how to structure con-versation! The Communities of Practice format is 100 percent what people need at this time. I'm now a believer. This format will produce the accelerated action we desire; much better than the lecture-style we've been doing. You've got the floor now."

Over the next two-and-a-half years, I led that cohort and many others like it, establishing the Communities of Practice format as a best practice for future cohorts managed by the contracting agency.

It's important to note that these cohorts wouldn't have been successful if I was the *only* one leading them. I needed the core planning team's technical expertise to identify key topics essential for advancing autonomous navigation systems that meet maritime safety standards. And they needed *me* to know how best to fuel the learning and reflection that would define those next steps and encourage follow-through. In the end, it was a good yin and yang partnership!

Your Challenge:
Stand Tall in Your Process Strengths

Believing the lie that you don't deserve a seat at the table because you're not a technical expert can trigger an instant, gut-level reaction. You might take a posture of "I'll show them," exhausting yourself trying to prove your worth. Or you might react with entitlement, feeling angry and resentful, convinced that you're unappreciated and undervalued.

In my story, I was 100 percent embodying *entitled* energy in those first few cohort connections. I wanted the team to respect me as a process expert. My frustration was rising and patience waning as my suggestions for cohort design were ini-tially tossed to the side. Oh, innovator, there was a raging war

The strength of process expertise is only valued **once someone has experienced it.**

of words happening inside my mind! However, I was smart enough to know that expressing that *entitled* energy was going to get me nowhere. Rather, I needed to tap into grounded and balanced energy, if I had a prayer of changing the dynamics at play within this team.

I called on that Care Bear image of love that I mentioned in the "On the Runway" chapter. I understood, and had empathy for, why my teammates were not trusting me to perform my role of cohort facilitator. In their minds, I had to be an expert on the topic of maritime safety and operational standards to lead people through a rich, reflective conversation on that topic. I knew that level of technical expertise was not needed, but they didn't. I had to be patient with them. Remember, the strength of process expertise is generally only valued once someone has experienced it.

To that end, I knew that I needed a shot at demonstrating my value as a process expert. Without that opportunity, my time was better spent elsewhere. To stay operating as the cohort's secretary felt like an irresponsible stewardship of the cohort's funds.

This realization pushed me into that tough conversation, which led to me being given the next cohort to facilitate. When I designed it around a Communities of Practice format, it completely changed the dynamic of the group—in the best way possible!

I want you, innovator, to stand in your strengths as a process expert as well . . . just as I did in the story that I shared. However, to do that with confidence, you need to be clear on your unique gifts as a process facilitator. Gaining clarity on those gifts, so that you can lead with love, compassion, and service at the forefront of your energy, is the focus of this chapter's challenge.

Accept the Challenge:
Define Your Superpowers

I believe we're all born with a superpower, a gift that makes each one of us truly unique in this world. This exercise, which was adapted from my business mentor, Heather Dominick, is all about defining and claiming your superpower gift(s), so that you can stand tall in the advocation of those gifts when you find yourself in situations like my story with the autonomous shipping cohort.

There are six steps to defining your superpower(s):

1. Identify some "in flow" shining moments

Think of three to five moments in your past when you've felt the most "in flow." These are moments when you have felt excited, passionate, and energized in what you're doing. Feel free to reference both personal and professional examples. Describe the instances in your life when you have found yourself having boundless energy for what you're working on, extreme mental clarity, or a deep sense of purpose and connection, for instance.

2. Write about each of those experiences

In a journal (it's important for it to be paper and pen—remember, energy flows differently on the page than on the screen), title each one of those experiences and write about it. Let the words flow.

Describe the event exhaustively: Who, if anyone else besides you, was there? What was the energy in the room? What were you doing? How were you feeling at that moment? How were the other people feeling at that moment?

3. Look for the patterns

Reread what you wrote about each experience. Which themes or patterns do you see? What, for you or others in the room, unlocked the "flow" in those moments?

4. Distill those patterns into a word or phrase

Choose a word or phrase that embodies the superpower gift(s) shining through. For instance, when I did this exercise for myself, the word *clarity* kept rising to the top to describe my "in flow" moments. Stories culminating in this word were about the following:

- My talents in synthesizing information in real time. I can listen to someone talk in circles (seemingly) for a given period of time and then, in three short sentences, say, "So, this is what I'm hearing you say…. Did I capture that accurately?" More times than not, people are like, "Yes, perfectly, and how did you do that?!"

- My love of facilitation. In my stories, I was struck by how natural and easy facilitation feels for me. It might be when I feel *the most alive* in my work. I love the discovery and learning that happens—for myself and others. And from a group management perspective, I intuitively know when to let the conversation wander a bit and then when to rein it back in, all in support of the desired growth of the engagement.

- My commitment to helping the people and organizations that I work with to show up as the best versions of themselves. I have the innate ability to home in on what will bring focus and purpose to the groups that I am working with, all while gracefully silencing the noise and chaos of the unimportant—the stuff that can easily take them off course from the growth they seek.

5. Try your superpower on for size

Interact with the world for a few days, witnessing how that word or phrase comes to life—both personally and professionally. Does the word that you've chosen properly characterize the unique value that you are offering to these situations? If anything feels uneasy about it, reflect on why. If that one doesn't feel quite right, go back to those initial patterns that you identified from your "in flow" stories and articulate another gift word or phrase to try on. Ideally, try to solidify one to three superpower gifts that stand out and resonate as unique to you.

6. Gather supporting evidence of your superpower in action

Lastly, I encourage you to track, in a methodical way, how your superpower is activated in your daily life. For a period of a few months, take notes on when your superpower shows up and the tangible value it offers to the situation or work that you're doing in that moment. (For convenience, I like to do this using the Notes app on my phone.) This tracking exercise supports you in building your confidence. The historical record of this exercise is also valuable. The content that you've captured can help to recenter you when you find yourself in situations where your competency as a process expert is questioned in a room full of technical experts.

This challenge presents a process for how you can become aware of, understand, and fully own your gifts as a process expert—so that you can advocate for them with strength and conviction—when needed. I'd be remiss if I didn't remind you, innovator, that fully embodying your expertise is a process. It does not happen overnight. So, my advice is *start now*.

What to Expect

You'll likely be dismissed from innovation work (probably more than once) given your lack of technical expertise. Just know that.

You can get caught up in the unproductive behaviors of "trying to prove your teammates wrong" or in lamenting, behind the scenes, how your counterparts "just don't understand or value you." But these pathways of brooding don't ultimately get you to where you want to be. They keep you stuck.

On the contrary, if you take the time to fully understand and own your strengths as a process expert, you'll have the confidence, when put in these situations, to speak to your value—and to give tangible examples of *how* that value has benefited other individuals and groups that you've had the privilege of serving in the past.

The stakeholders that you're working with will, more times than not, respond positively when you are centered and confident in the communication of your gifts. If you have a clear ask, like I did in suggesting that I facilitate the next cohort meeting, your teammates will often back off just enough to give you the space to do your thing. And this is your opening to show *how* your process expertise can support the actions and broader goals of the group.

I encourage you to make your ask a low-barrier one... something the team can bounce back from if the experiment of you using your gifts in this way turns out to be a royal disaster. For instance, if that one Communities of Practice cohort discussion had been a miss, the net result of that entire initiative would not have been jeopardized. It would have been remembered as an unfavorable glitch, at most.

Also, importantly, build into your ask a designated time to regroup for a reflection on the value of your gifts to the broader goals of the initiative. This is a debrief that you'll want to facilitate sometime within twenty-four hours after your teammates have seen your process gifts in action. You do not want this conversation to take the tone of "I told you so..." Instead, focus on building a connection that helps your teammates see how your unique skills complement theirs. This brings the full strength of the team together to drive the project's broader goals forward.

Mindset Shift: Stand Tall in Your Process Strengths

Process expertise is valued and appreciated only once a person experiences it. You can whine about that and further shadow your value, or you can be proactive in defining the process superpowers that you possess and the tangible benefits they offer to the people you work with. Start defining your unique process strengths now. Doing so will support you in advocating for them with conviction and confidence the next time your contribution to a team is brought into question.

10

Watch Your Frog

SUFFOCATING—that's how I feel when projects start to fall into fatigue. The exhaustion creeps up until I can't take it anymore and just want to scream, "Enough!" It's like slowly boiling a frog (not that I've tried that).

The metaphor goes like this: A frog will jump out of boiling water to escape danger, but if placed in lukewarm water that's slowly heated, it won't notice the gradual change and will stay until it's too late. Its adaptability—usually a strength—becomes its downfall.

Now, I consider myself to be a pretty adaptable leader. Generally, this is a positive trait, one that helps me lead projects that encourage teamwork and shared decision-making. I take the expectations of my clients to heart, making every effort to meet their needs. In most cases, this is a good thing . . . until it's not.

And that is the crux of the problem. When you, as an innovation leader, are in the thick of a project, responding to existing and emerging requirements, it can be difficult to pinpoint the moment when you and your team are about to be "boiled"— when the demands of your clients have reached a point where your ability to be successful in the initiative is questioned.

You become aware of the fact that you have been "boiled" only after it has happened, once you're dealing with the trickle-down impacts of a team with decreased morale, productivity, and trust, when internal team conflicts have increased, or you're dealing with higher turnover than normal.

This chapter, dear innovator, is about helping you avoid the "boiled frog" fate; it's about helping you be more tuned into your own needs as an innovation leader so that you can more accurately discern when team dynamics have shifted from a space of collaboration to one of submission and micromanagement.

What It Looks Like

We were working on a multiphase service design project. This initiative had several C-suite eyes on it, which meant that the anxiety around the project was elevated. Our core stakeholders responded to this amplified pressure by inserting more checkpoints into the work process.

My core client team wanted to connect every few days as we analyzed and synthesized the research data that had been collected. In their words, they "wanted to stay close to the data and collaborate on how the insights came to life" for their stakeholders. Yet, they didn't have the bandwidth to get into the weeds of analyzing and synthesizing the data themselves.

When they proposed this checkpoint scheme, I wasn't 100 percent comfortable with it. I knew, from past experience, that my team and I needed time to sit with data and work with it iteratively—over the course of a few weeks—before an impactful storyline usually takes shape. But I wanted to be a good partner, and it was clear that my clients needed more control and transparency at that moment. So, despite my misgivings, I obliged.

We began the analysis and synthesis process of our work and started connecting with our key client stakeholders every two days. Yet, after two of these checkpoints, it was obvious we had made a mistake by saying yes to this request. Our client came to these meetings with an unspoken expectation that we would deliver a clear part of "the answer" at each of these connections—something finessed enough to be worthy of executive consumption. But we just weren't there yet; we were still making sense of the data. Worse, with every meeting, we were losing ground toward the bigger goal of creating a deliverable that *was* worthy of executive consumption. We were spending too much time preparing for the next checkpoint, ultimately doing work that wasn't necessarily useful or productive toward our actual project deliverables.

And because our client wasn't seeing that deliverable worthy of executive consumption at each checkpoint, their anxiety intensified. This led to them injecting even more control and micromanagement into the process. They insisted that we complete certain parts of the deliverable with each subsequent checkpoint. And the vitality of my team took a nosedive.

We no longer felt we had autonomy in how we did our work or how we produced the outcome we knew we were responsible for—and capable of—providing. With every checkpoint, we felt the client was questioning our ability to deliver the executive presentation we had agreed to. This didn't feel collaborative at all; we weren't working with or for one another.

As the leader of this team, I was barely surviving. My stress was through the roof, and I felt closed in. I needed two weeks of space and time to bring this deliverable to life, time to think and be creative. Instead, I felt suffocated by my client, who was looming large over us. I also felt guilty. This project was not only impacting my vitality, but also obliterating the engagement and productivity of my broader team. It was a cluster that only got worse with each day.

I started to fantasize about quitting the project altogether, handing back the money the client had paid. That's when I knew something had to give. We were only partway through this multiphase project. We had many months ahead of us, and I knew we couldn't continue down the path we were on. Hence, a difficult conversation was in order.

Now to state the obvious: The thing about difficult conversations is that you never really want to have them. But being the leader of my team meant that I needed to pull up my big-girl pants in support of restoring the vitality of my team and the quality of our client relationship. I really, really, *really* didn't want to engage in this dialogue, but I felt that I had no other choice. If we didn't change the client dynamic happening, we wouldn't make it to the finish line of this initiative and, quite possibly, some of my team members would leave Sylver Consulting altogether. I had to act.

Before I approached a conversation with my clients, however, I needed to be crystal clear on what my team and I needed to reclaim our energy and excitement for this project. We had an internal discussion and determined we needed an end to the micromanagement. We needed time and freedom to create, fewer check-in calls, and more control in communicating when our content was presentation-ready and available for feedback and iteration.

Armed with this insight, I sat down with our clients. I led with empathy and understanding as I began this conversation. (Yes—I was fully embodying that Care Bear of love imagery as I entered this dialogue.) I said, "I understand why you're asking for more checkpoints on this project, compared to others. I also understand that this is a big project for your organization and that a lot is on the line for you professionally related to it. You don't want to be in the dark; I get that. But the way we're working right now is not working for my team and me, and the success of our project—and our relationship—is at risk because of it."

I told them—kindly and honestly—how my team was experiencing the checkpoints. I shared that these iterative meetings were preventing the very goal we were all striving for, which was a polished deliverable worthy of executive consumption. I admitted that we were bringing half-baked ideas to each checkpoint because we lacked time to fully process the data—leaving us discussing feedback on work no one felt proud of.

Then I asked my client what was going on from their perspective. What did they feel was working about the checkpoints and what was not? I also asked them to tell me more about what they were hoping to get out of these regular meetings.

I discovered that their deepest concern was being caught off guard by the results. This particular initiative would feed many other projects within the organization. They didn't want to find themselves in the dark, uncertain of how to lead and coach other members of their organization on how to use the insights most effectively. This made sense to me.

I reminded them that our goal was the same—to deliver amazing insight that would enable growth for the organization. I also shared that to do this and hit all of our deadlines, my team needed more space and autonomy to create. Together, we came up with an even more detailed and specific timeline for the work; however, this time that calendar was co-created—not dictated—and it aligned with the cycle of our natural work rhythms as a team (which was not every two business days).

At last, my team had the space we needed to create, and my clients had clear expectations for what they would receive at each checkpoint. The checkpoints began to fuel forward momentum in our work together, we were doing a lot less rework, and we stuck to that co-created timeline for the duration of the project. Ultimately, we were able to restore the relationship and get back to a place where my team was engaged in the work and felt capable of achieving the success metrics we had for it. But we wouldn't have reached that point if I had not been brave enough to engage in that difficult conversation.

Your Challenge: Prioritize Vitality

This challenge, innovator, is about periodically taking the temperature of you and your team, so that you can better catch when the temperatures are rising to such a degree that you and your partnerships are at risk of being boiled.

We can look to the self-determination theory of psychologists Richard Ryan and Edward Deci as inspiration for how to gain that "temperature check." Ryan and Deci found that humans have three basic needs: autonomy, competence, and relatedness. When these basic needs are met, people are motivated to grow and change and have the capacity to realize their full potential. The degree to which each of these basic human needs is satisfied impacts vitality levels. Vitality can be described as the fuel or energy that drives or powers a person's thoughts, actions, and emotions.

When the basic needs of autonomy, competence, and relatedness are met for you and your team, your vitality is high, which means you and your team are positioned for success. You're firing on all cylinders, engaged in the work, and committed to producing standout outcomes.

In contrast, when the basic needs of autonomy, competence, and relatedness are not being met for you and your team, your vitality is low, which means you and your team are *not*

Your responsibility as a leader of innovation **is to fiercely protect the vitality of both you and your team.**

positioned for success. You lack enthusiasm and engagement in your work. You're going through the motions, oftentimes losing sight of what it looks like to create impactful and meaningful output in your work. You might complete the work, but the result is adequate to sub-par. You're surviving the project, not thriving in it.

Your responsibility as a leader of innovation is to fiercely protect the vitality of both you and your team. To support you in doing that, I encourage you to check in with yourself and your team each month with these three Vitality Pulse questions. Go project by project, asking each question for each project that you're managing or are engaged in.

Related to the basic need of autonomy, ask yourself: *Do I feel like I* want to do *this project or like I* have to do *this project?* When you or your team begin to feel pressured or forced, like you *have to* work on a project versus being excited that you *get to* work on a project, that's a red flag needing attention. As humans, we need to feel that we have ownership and agency over our own behavior; otherwise, our effectiveness dims.

Related to the basic need of competency, ask yourself: *Do I feel skilled and able to do this project successfully?* When you and your team begin to feel ineffective, or like you can't achieve a specific outcome in your work, vitality wanes. You begin to feel helpless. And, again, your effectiveness will dim.

Related to the basic need of relatedness, ask yourself: *Am I surrounded by supportive relationships and people who understand me and want me to succeed?* When you and your team begin to feel lonely, isolated, misunderstood, or excluded, this is a warning bell. As humans, we need to feel a sense of attachment and connectedness to others; otherwise, once again, our effectiveness dims.

Do you see the pattern here, innovator? If you fail to protect your vitality and the collective energy of your team, then you're *consciously choosing* to dim your light and to compromise your effectiveness.

Back to the boiling-frog metaphor. It's easy to find yourself slowly cooked before you've realized the hot water that you've gotten yourself into. Why? Because if, like me, you're committed to *collaboration* as a core value, you naturally embrace flexibility and adaptability in response to changing circumstances, priorities, and opportunities. You value being able and willing to adjust plans, roles, and strategies as needed, as you've seen that behavior, in the past, promote team resilience and support teams to seize new opportunities for innovation.

This level of flexibility and adaptation is good ... until it's not. These three Vitality Pulse questions will help you discern when you've got an energy problem on your hands that needs attention.

And when the warning sirens blare, this is your invitation for a difficult conversation. Read on to see what it looks like to engage in that uncomfortable—yet über important—dialogue.

Accept the Challenge:
Embrace the Difficult Conversation

Now, friends, in my story, I was "boiled" long before I came to the realization that I needed to pursue a difficult conversation with my clients. I want your path to restoration to be much smoother than my own.

To avoid the boiled-frog fate, establish a regular practice of checking your Vitality Pulse, as discussed earlier in this chapter. When you find that your energy or your team's energy is at risk, pull all relevant parties together to address the matter head-on, using the discussion guide shared below. This conversation is simple in theory and setup, but perhaps less straightforward when it comes to managing your own feelings throughout the conversation.

When you do get everyone in the room, it's important to control your tone in the conversation, being careful to avoid any timbre of accusation. You're there simply to acknowledge that vitality is low and to give voice to the dynamics creating that sense of drain—for yourself and others. Your goal is to emerge from this discussion with ideas. *What next-step actions might be taken to change the team dynamics happening, for the positive?* Ideally, the solution is co-created: something that all parties agree on.

Despite the fact that your goal is to emerge from this conversation with a co-created solution, it's important that you enter the dialogue with ideas for how you might change the negative team dynamic for the better. Having these ideas as thought starters can accelerate the restorative value of this difficult conversation.

As I mentioned earlier, the actual structure of this conversation is simple, following six steps:

1   Thank your partners for entering into this dialogue with you.

2   Verbally acknowledge that your vitality is low. Be as specific as you can about what is causing that drain in energy for yourself and the cascading impacts of that lack of energy on your project. When I engaged in this difficult conversation with my clients, I knew that the iterative review schedule was the root of much of the discomfort that I was feeling. I also felt that the frequency of the review connections were taking my team and me further away from the deliverable goals promised of our project.

3. Seek to understand your partner's side of the story. Once you've shared your feelings, give them space to explain how they are experiencing the dynamic at play. *What is working about the situation for them and what is not?*
4. Suggest some solutions for how you might change—for the positive—the current team dynamic. Again, I recommend that you have initial ideas on what you'd like to see changed before going into this conversation. However, also be willing to adjust those ideas based on your dialogue.
5. Co-create next steps that can be taken, in the hopes of restoring the relationship and refueling everyone's vitality. The next steps should promise to support and satisfy both parties' needs.
6. Set the expectation that you'll check in to see how the next steps are working for everyone. The time duration for that check-in will be customized based on the next steps defined.

What to Expect

When I know one of these conversations is on the horizon, I don't sleep well the night before. It stirs all sorts of anxiety because, let's face it, these conversations aren't fun.

These dialogues are difficult and uncomfortable because, while you may go into this conversation intent on being grounded and centered throughout it, you can't predict how your partners in the dialogue will respond to you. There's a possibility that you'll be verbally attacked in return, despite being on your best behavior! I bring this possibility up so that you can do the prep work required to disarm and prevent this assault as much as possible.

Energetically, this means consciously discharging any defensiveness that you might be holding in your heart *before* you enter this conversation. I know this is easier said than done, but these conversations really do go better when you lead them with a softened and open heart. (Remember the Care Bear shining love from its belly! Embody that imagery.)

Also, as prep work for this conversation, it is important to clarify how the current team dynamic affects your energy (or your team's) and identify initial steps to create a more positive outcome for everyone.

Most of the time, these conversations turn out well—you find a compromise or a new way of working together that feels good for everyone involved. But sometimes, they don't. Even then, take pride in the fact that you've stood up for yourself. You're on a path to greater energy and fulfillment, even if it means moving on.

The last thing to note is that this conversation is rarely a one-and-done type of deal. It's an important milestone on a journey, but it's not the endpoint. You'll likely need to circle back with your dialogue partners, to check in on whether the new plan is working for both of you. And these later conversations might lead you to a different plan or approach, especially if it's a multiphase endeavor.

Mindset Shift: Prioritize Vitality

It's your responsibility to fiercely protect vitality. The effectiveness of your work and team depends on it. Commit to frequently checking your Vitality Pulse. When dips are experienced, address them. First, reflect: *Why am I feeling this way and what might be done differently to change the situation?* Then, engage in the difficult conversations to get down to the brass tacks: *What next steps will be taken to restore my vitality and refuel the energy of my team?*

11

Evolve in Real Time

EVERY GOOD INNOVATOR starts with a plan: a clear starting point, a defined end goal, and a vision for the path to get from point A to point B. If you're Type A like me, you live for these project plans. They're your anchor. Each milestone hit and task checked off delivers that sweet dopamine rush, as progress unfolds and your vision takes shape.

So, what happens, innovator, when your plan stops delivering?

These are the moments when you hear *the voice* that whispers, "Maybe it's time to pivot?" It's that nagging sense that maybe, just maybe, your original plan isn't quite on point. Something feels off; your outcomes are no longer aligned to what the project or market really needs—or maybe even your own vision for the project has evolved. That feeling? It's a sign that something isn't right. You've got to choose, innovator: Do you listen to *the voice* or ignore it?

Inside, you're torn. On one side, there's comfort with your original plan and the feeling that you must continue because you've already invested so much in this plan, from a time and resources perspective. On the other, there is this creeping realization that sticking to the script might actually lead to project failure.

The thought of change stirs up fear: fear of the unknown, fear of what others might think, fear of admitting that the first idea wasn't flawless. To pivot, you've got to let go of that attachment, set aside your ego, and take a leap into the unknown. It's about trusting your gut, being flexible, and keeping your eyes on the bigger picture, even when it means stepping off the well-worn path.

What It Looks Like

We were knee-deep in a four-phase process to help our client carve out a distinct place in the market—if I may draw on the Red Ocean/Blue Ocean contrast coined by Chan Kim and Renée Mauborgne, my client wanted a market space free from the intense competition of their industry's Red Ocean. The goal was to chart a course into the Blue Ocean, where the waters were clear, and the competition irrelevant. But as we neared the end of the third phase, what should have been Blue Ocean territory was looking more like a murky shade of purple.

The executive team had started viewing the Blue Ocean opportunity as merely a new product launch. Yet, the market was telling us that a new product alone wouldn't cut it. What my client needed was a more radical approach—a restructuring of their business model, a reshaping of their marketing strategies, and a realignment of their resources. Capturing the Blue Ocean wasn't just about the development of a new product. It was about reinventing the way my client did business.

I started to hear *the voice*—that nagging feeling in my gut telling me that we were off course. We were close to the finish line of the project (from a timeline perspective), yet so far from the goal of a Blue Ocean vision. So, I did the uncomfortable thing: I brought my concerns to my client.

This was not a decision that I came to with ease. This was the first time that we were working with this client. I had sold them a project plan that looked good on paper, a project plan that I was confident would deliver the desired results when we set out on this journey. However, that plan was not delivering.

In a lot of ways, I felt that I had failed my client. Shame was gnawing at my heart. We were deep into the project, and I was about to say, "I don't think we're set up for success."

Logically speaking, I knew that I shouldn't feel the shame that I did. We had learned a ton about the mindset of the market in the prior three phases of work, insights that were challenging core ingoing hypotheses of the initiative. We also now knew our client a lot more—their capabilities, mindsets, and willingness to take market risks. Essentially, the landscape that we were innovating in was evolving in real time and that uneasy feeling in the pit of my stomach was telling me that our project needed to as well. So, at our next weekly checkpoint, I broached the subject of a pivot with our client.

To my surprise, she was relieved. She'd been feeling that same unease. Over the next hour, we unpacked our concerns. We realized that we weren't just offtrack; we were at a crossroads.

We had uncovered more about the Red Ocean dynamics than expected. While some promising paths toward the Blue Ocean vision emerged, the executive team lacked confidence in deciding which path to follow. Upon receiving this information, my team and I suggested that we pivot the fourth phase of the work. We landed on facilitating a workshop using LEGO® SERIOUS PLAY® methodology to define which Blue Ocean pathway was going to be most effective for our client.

In a workshop using LEGO SERIOUS PLAY methodology, participants use LEGO® bricks to create business strategy. The 3D nature of the project breaks the script on how members of

To pivot, you've got to let go of that attachment, set aside your ego, **and take a leap into the unknown.**

the organization understand the problem and what's possible in pursuit of solving that business challenge.

After we made our case for this workshop, my main client was on board—but we still needed buy-in from her broader stakeholder team. A series of meetings occurred to secure that buy-in. Four weeks later, we were executing the workshop.

In that workshop, each team member built models to respond to three prompt questions:

1 Who and what is your organization?
2 What's your business environment like?
3 What, then, is your Blue Ocean vision for tomorrow?

Each model, radically different from the others, helped the team understand the complexities of the market and the pockets of opportunity available in it. It highlighted the commitment it would take for our client to access the future Blue Ocean vision that they (and the market) desired. And it also humbled them. There were a lot of opportunities that they were leaving on the table yet in the Red Ocean.

Had my client and I not had the courage to hit pause on this initiative when we did—had we not listened to *the voice* nudging us to pivot—the project would have been a failure. Instead, it was a success, and a longstanding client partnership was born as a result.

Your Challenge: Assess if You're Meant to Adapt

Innovator, that *voice* in your head . . . it's your friend. It's challenging you to pause and ask: *Are you meant to stay the course or pivot?*

And that *voice* is demanding a direct answer from you: "Do you believe that you can meet the goals of your project, if you stay the course?"

If the answer is yes, you're golden. Keep on keeping on.

If the answer is a maybe or a no, it's time to go in for a deeper inquiry (ideally in partnership with your team).

Tactically speaking, this looks like giving yourself and your team a couple of hours to fully assess what is or has happened in the project. *Why has the caution flag been raised by your intuition?* In this conversation, you want to

- weigh the strengths and weaknesses of your current planned strategy, in light of the new information;

- ideate how else you might approach the project to increase your success confidence;

- evaluate those new, emergent plans, assessing their strengths and weaknesses, compared to your original approach.

Does it make sense to pivot? If the answer is yes, then lean in to define the pivot execution plan:

- Who needs to buy into this change in approach?

- What steps are needed to gain their support?

- What shifts are required to work process and product to enable the pivot?

- Are there any impacts on the budget or timeline?

As you dig into this assessment, I pray that you leave any feelings of shame, guilt, or fear behind. The innovation process is dynamic. Sometimes new information (about the market, industry competitors, or even your own organization's capabilities, strengths, and weaknesses) demands a midair adjustment. I'm granting you permission to make last-minute changes to plans based on new information or circumstances.

Accept the Challenge:
Call the Midair Adjustments

Let's level set here—no one *plans* to be in this moment, questioning all that's laid out in front of them. The moment itself is inconvenient, to say the least. However, as the innovator navigating this moment, you get to choose the attitude you bring to it. It's my hope that you embrace these challenging moments with resilience and positivity.

I pray that you resist the temptation to internalize this need for course correction as an overwhelming setback, as something to apologize for or be irritated and frustrated by. Choosing this posture will only further leave you rudderless and listless.

You can't change the new information you've discovered or the new hand you've been dealt. You do get to choose, however, if you opt for an attitude of adaptability and openness. My hope is that you learn to accept this challenge with open arms.

Making the decision to pivot away from a planned strategy, which you've gained buy-in and alignment around, is not a trivial proposition. In fact, it's likely to trigger an internal "Oh, crap!" type of response because you know that pivoting away from the planned strategy means more work for you: more meetings, more paperwork, changes to timelines and resources ... the list goes on.

But beneath that dread of more work, there's a deeper knowing. You're not going to get to where everybody needs to be if you continue down the current path. You're not going to be a good steward of the money, the time, or the people involved.

So, here's your challenge, innovator—it's time to feel that weight of responsibility and pull the ripcord. Don't apologize if things aren't going according to plan. Sometimes, it's the turbulence that guides us to a clearer landing.

What to Expect

The most uncomfortable part of this activity is the acknowledgment that you've heard *the voice* and can no longer unhear it. You're being called to act.

It's definitely tempting to ignore *this voice*; staying the course requires a lot less work of you, after all. But pursuing that route is an act of cowardness. *The voice* is speaking to you: "If you don't change direction, you may end up where you are heading." And you know that is *not* where you want to be.

The only way you're going to get to a different, better outcome is to be brave and champion the course corrections that you know, in your heart, are needed. Feel the feels that you will, for a moment—the feelings that make you question if you did something wrong. And then let that go. Circumstances have changed. You are smarter today than you were yesterday, and the new information is demanding a new approach.

The longer you wrestle with the conflicting feelings of needing to change course but avoid the decision to act, the more anxious you'll feel. Staying stuck in indecision doesn't help your project. The more you delay, the further you stray from the path to a successful outcome.

You see, the second you acknowledge the presence of the unease, you defang it. It's no longer a deficiency of the project, you, your team, or your project stakeholders. It's simply an issue that needs collective attention and problem-solving, an issue that's evolved in real time as you've executed your project in real life.

So, I invite you, innovator, to lean into that assessment conversation, get clear on if you're meant to adapt, and have the courage to advocate for the midair course corrections when the answer is yes.

Sometimes, you'll be met with relief when you voice a concern—often because you've put words to something others have felt but haven't been able to express. Other times, you may face resistance. In these moments, take a deep breath and lead with patience. While you've had time to process your thoughts, the person you're speaking with likely hasn't. Give them space to catch up, and you can help by clearly sharing your assessment and reasoning.

Mindset Shift: Assess if You're Meant to Adapt

You know what they say about the best-laid plans—they don't always go as expected. When your path suddenly takes an unexpected turn, be ready to adjust. Sometimes you'll choose to stay the course. Other times, you'll make a mid-project course correction. The key is knowing what call to make when.

12

Weather the Blamestorm

CALL IT a "blamestorm"—the moment when you suddenly become the scapegoat, the target of finger-pointing for everything that's gone wrong. It often hits you out of nowhere. There you are, just doing your job: exploring market dynamics and organizational nuances to find growth opportunities for your stakeholders. But then you stumble upon a fault line—a problem, issue, weakness, or gap—that the very people you're trying to help would rather keep hidden. Their knee-jerk reaction? Shoot the messenger—and that's you. Oof!

You can discover—or stumble upon—all sorts of fault lines in innovation work: strategic, operational, technical, financial, cultural, leadership-oriented, and market-related, among others. The common thread is that those involved in your work prefer for these problems, issues, weaknesses, or gaps to remain hidden. Yet, once these challenges are exposed, they become impossible to ignore.

Dealing with these challenges is something your stakeholders aren't prepared for. You've told the truth (a noble thing). Yet, your stakeholders, as they receive this message, experience cognitive dissonance, meaning the new information conflicts with existing beliefs, thoughts, or expectations, causing your stakeholders to reel in response.

153

You often experience this moment as grenades of hate and incompetence being lobbed at you, your team, and your processes. Did you do anything wrong to get yourself here? Nope. You just did your job. Does that change how you experience this moment? Nope, it sure does not.

Your stakeholders need to let go of their previous beliefs to embrace the new insights your work has revealed. This can be an emotional journey (akin to a grief journey), and your role as the innovator is to guide them through it. The key challenge is to remain grounded and not lose yourself in the process.

What It Looks Like

At first glance, this messaging project seemed simple enough. A few years prior, a personal care company had switched to a new strategic messaging framework for its brand. According to the RFP, market messaging aligned to this framework had been performing well, with sales on the rise. The company was considering a few adjustments to its market messaging and wanted to test the waters on it before moving forward.

Great! I thought. *An easy project.*

We began the work, which included both quantitative and qualitative research. As data began to roll in, alarm sirens started to wail.

Quantitative research revealed *significant* room for improvement in the new messaging for this consumer brand. My client's messaging was evaluated against other consumer ads, focusing on metrics like clarity and understanding, appeal, relevance, uniqueness, believability, purchase intent, and perceived value. Unfortunately, the messaging fell below the industry benchmark in six out of seven categories! It wasn't the strong, differentiating, and unique market message the team thought they had. Ouch!

The qualitative conversations were adding context and color to these results. The messaging slogan elicited praise and intrigue from consumers. However, quick on the heels of that excitement was the question "How?" In short, the believability of the brand's message was in question.

I knew these results were not what my client ideally wanted to hear. However, I was completely blindsided by what came next.

We presented the results to two groups of stakeholders. The first group was thrilled, with one key stakeholder saying, "This is excellent work; it's easy to execute and act on. It's more than I expected when we started." Another stakeholder, in that same meeting, added, "This is why we hire you. You always deliver."

We felt proud as a team. We clearly communicated the gaps in our client's market message without triggering defensiveness. Even better, the plan we laid out to close those gaps felt practical and doable by our stakeholders. Success!

Or so we thought...

Just hours later, we met with a second group of stakeholders—the people who held the financial reins of the strategic messaging framework for the brand. As we walked them through the same presentation, I could almost see the warning lights flashing in their heads by the time we hit slide 3. Their reactions were visceral; faces tightened, and tension filled the room. It was clear their limbic systems were in overdrive, grappling with the potential financial and timeline chaos a shift in the brand's messaging would create. The fear of being held accountable for those consequences was written all over their expressions. Their response was swift and emphatic: "No way. Not on our watch."

It felt like whiplash. The first group was thrilled, seeing clear, actionable ways to boost the brand's performance across all benchmarks. In stark contrast, the second group of stakeholders regretted the project entirely. They quickly huddled with my main client contact (who had been part of that first stakeholder group). My team was not asked to be part of that discussion. Definitely not a good sign.

A few hours later, I received an updated presentation. The client had made several changes to downplay the negative feedback from the research. Key underperforming metrics were removed, and the executive summary now highlighted irrelevant but positive stats, rather than addressing the message's poor performance.

As I reviewed the revised deck, I was stunned. My client had been eager to benchmark their work against other brands of the industry—until they realized it fell short. Now, they wanted to dilute the findings to save face with their executive leadership. I was stuck in a tough spot. The client was on the verge of dismissing my team and had already decided we wouldn't present to another group of stakeholders. They were determined to control the narrative.

I was upset but walking away wasn't an option. My job as the lead innovator was to shine a light on these issues, not to let them be swept back under the rug. Recognizing this, I knew I had to approach the situation with compassion—to find a middle ground that worked for both sides. So, I reached out to my main client contact to discuss the next steps.

"I can see these results have stirred up some anxiety," I said gently. "I've looked over the revised presentation. I'm on board with some changes but have reservations about others. Let's pause and discuss why we're seeing such different reactions to the insights today." My client was open to the discussion.

My first question was, "What specific new information is causing your stakeholders the most concern?" It turned out that their brand message not meeting industry benchmarks was sparking anxiety.

My next question was, "So, what happens if your brand message doesn't meet or exceed industry benchmarks?" The client outlined the potential sunk costs and timeline delays they'd face if they had to change their market message. She also mentioned that making those changes with the current budget and timeline felt impossible.

I pressed further: "What might happen if your leaders learn that the current messaging lacks the punch that you thought it had, and that current budgets and timelines might not allow for the full course correction needed? What about that situation creates unease?" It turned out the issue was less about the money and more about the prospect of regrouping and realigning the leadership team in a new direction. The team wasn't keen on starting from scratch.

I asked a fourth question: "Why does 'starting from scratch' feel overwhelming?" My client explained the long approval process of the organization and the likelihood that they would miss some crucial, nonnegotiable dates on the calendar if they decided to start over.

I now knew the root of my stakeholder's concerns. And we now had the information on the table that would help us to ultimately define the "third way"—an alternative solution that would meet the needs of all involved.

After an hour of productive conversation, we had formulated a plan, defining how to present our findings truthfully yet sensitively, taking into account our stakeholders' concerns. We agreed to reintroduce the benchmark statistics into the presentation and refine our language around the effectiveness of the brand message. We proposed using the upcoming workshop (the next step of our project plan) to explore how market feedback could influence both the current and future brand messaging strategies.

By the end of our conversation, my client was feeling more emotionally stable and prepared to advocate for the project's insights, despite the challenging results—which she did.

Ultimately, our client chose to proceed with the current brand message due to tight timelines and budget constraints. However, the insights we gathered were not in vain. The organization took them seriously and used them to overhaul the entire strategic messaging framework for the brand for the following year.

Your Challenge: Lead with Compassion

The first thing you've got to understand is this: If you're living up to your changemaker status as an innovator, you *will* experience moments like this.

In my career to date, I've had stakeholders ask me to "cook the books," to make sure certain concepts win in testing, for instance. I've had people request that I explicitly remove unfavorable data from reports, wanting only to focus on the positive and avoid highlighting any challenges. I've been uninvited to major presentations, so stakeholders could present the work with a narrative that downplayed the severity of their situation and because they feared I might say or do something to make the situation worse. I've also had stakeholders ask me to reprocess data, through a new lens or metric of success, in hopes that the outcome would be more favorable to the direction they wanted to lead the organization.

These situations are incredibly uncomfortable, fraught with moral and ethical dilemmas. You're faced with a choice:

Do you uphold the truth and maintain the integrity of your work, or do you compromise to gain immediate benefits like support or funding? It's tempting to claim, "I would *never* compromise my integrity!" Yet, that, innovator, is what we call "binary thinking." There is a way for you to embrace the complexity of a situation like this, while still communicating the truth. I propose that you look for a "third way."

Let's compare this to remodeling a home. You start with a clear vision, a planned process, and specific outcomes in mind. But as you dive into the renovation, you uncover a host of issues: rotten framing, foundation problems, outdated electrical systems, corroded plumbing, lead paint, hidden mold, and even termites. Each discovery adds complexity and scale to what was once a straightforward, and within budget, project. Suddenly, you're overwhelmed, forced to prioritize which issues need immediate attention and which can be temporarily set aside. This is the reality of innovation—navigating between immediate challenges and long-term goals, seeking solutions that honor both integrity and practicality.

My stakeholders, in the case study I just gave, had mentally prepared themselves for a quick polish of their market message—maybe a fresh coat of paint and a floor refinish. Instead, I had to tell them their foundation was cracked, and what they really needed was a complete renovation.

At moments like these, your stakeholders are in overdrive; their limbic systems have been taken hostage by stress. Their instinct might be to ignore the problems, cover them up, or dismiss those who have highlighted them. You face a choice: You can either stand your ground and fight for integrity at all costs, or you can lead with compassion and seek a balanced both/and solution.

Sometimes, an organization just isn't ready to tackle the larger issues that come to light. That's understandable. What

Your role is to guide your stakeholders through the processing of unexpected issues, **helping them navigate the five stages of grief.**

isn't acceptable, however, is ignoring these emerging fault lines or trying to hide them again. Nevertheless, it's perfectly reasonable for your stakeholders to decide not to tackle a specific issue, problem, or weakness right away.

Your primary role is to guide your stakeholders through the processing of unexpected issues, helping them navigate the five stages of grief, inclusive of denial, anger, bargaining, and depression before they ultimately get to a place of acceptance.

What this journey might look like, step by step, is detailed below:

1   **Denial:** Your stakeholders will refuse to accept the problems, issues, weaknesses, or gaps that have been brought to the surface in your work.

2   **Anger:** They'll direct blame toward you or your project team when those challenges and shortcomings have been highlighted. Your competence as a professional and the soundness of your project decisions is likely to be attacked. (Participant sample quality and methodology rigor are usually easy targets.)

3   **Bargaining:** Your stakeholders will want to downplay the fault lines that have been exposed, perhaps even outright asking for you to avoid conveying those issues in any formal project documentation (or to seriously downplay them if they are included).

4   **Depression:** Fear will be clouding your stakeholders' judgment, making it difficult for them to accept new truths. They may feel overwhelmed, sad, or disheartened, fearing they'll be held accountable for the issues you've uncovered.

5 **Acceptance:** This is the moment when your stakeholders come to terms with the exposed fault lines, when they finally acknowledge the need for change and start to explore constructive solutions for how to address the vulnerabilities that have surfaced.

Accept the Challenge: Get to the Root of the Defense

Your first task, when caught in a blamestorm, is to resist the urge to be defensive yourself. Remember, when both sides react with heightened emotions, rash decisions follow. It takes someone with a clear head and steady hands to steer through the chaos—you're intended to be that steadfast person, innovator.

As your stakeholders are traversing the first three steps of their grief journey (denial, anger, and bargaining), you will be triggered. Hold back, though, from reacting defensively when faced with harsh criticism and accusations of incompetence. Instead, take your stakeholders' defensiveness as a signal to deepen the dialogue. They are grieving. What they once believed to be true has been proven false. They need time to adjust to the new reality.

The most effective way you can assist them—and yourself—is by helping them to process their defensive feelings. This approach not only mitigates the conflict but also accelerates their journey from denial to acceptance.

Four questions will help you unlock "third way" options—innovative, alternative approaches that go beyond binary options—when in these situations:

1 What specific new information is causing the most concern for you and your stakeholders?

2   What could be the potential outcomes of this concern?

3   What might happen if others were to discover these potential outcomes?

4   Why does the possibility of these outcomes feel overwhelming to you?

These questions—when facilitated with compassion and nonjudgement—will deepen your understanding of your stakeholders' discomfort and anxiety and give clarity to what "third way" solutions might work—solutions that will honor the truth that has emerged in the research and the time that the organization needs to adjust to that new truth.

When you get to brainstorming "third way" options, use this guiding question: "How might we share the truth of what we learned, while honoring your concerns around X, Y, and Z?" (Here X, Y, and Z represent the specific concerns and consequences identified in the earlier questions).

After generating various "third way" options, identify the most effective path forward. These should allow you to highlight the critical issues you've discovered while enabling your stakeholders to strategically decide whether and how to address them. Your role, throughout this process, is to support your stakeholders in making thoughtful and informed decisions on how to respond to the new truths that have emerged from your work.

What to Expect

The blamestorm is a tempest of emotions—it's destructive, hurtful, and sometimes downright terrifying. It's all too easy to lose your bearings, to forget who you are and overlook the humanity of those caught in the storm with you. Getting sucked into this storm will lead only to suffering, and it certainly won't help you embody the servant leader you aspire to be. Instead of charging into battle, you must strive to rise above it.

To successfully "rise above the battle," it's essential to first find your emotional footing. Remember, there's no pressure to react immediately. If you need time to process your feelings, take it. The conversations I'm encouraging you to lead demand a high level of emotional intelligence, and for that, you need to be in the right heart space. Allow yourself some grace. Most people require a moment to recenter themselves. Take that necessary pause, regroup, and then engage in the dialogue with clarity and compassion.

The flow of your dialogue with stakeholders will vary depending on the trust established in your relationship. The stronger the trust, the smoother the conversation will flow. It's important to understand this dynamic—not as a judgment but as a context for navigating the discussion. In situations where trust might be lower, you may need to probe deeper to uncover the reasons behind any defensiveness toward your work.

As you work through the four questions, you'll begin to feel more grounded and open. Your confusion, and the betrayal you might be feeling, will start to dissipate, making way for "third way" solutions to emerge. This clarity will not only benefit you but also help your stakeholders. As they observe their own reactions from this refreshed perspective, they too will start to ease, opening up to new possibilities and collaborative solutions.

The ultimate goal is to come out of this dialogue with a solution that everyone feels positive about. We're aiming for that "third way" approach that respects the work and the real constraints around it.

Mindset Shift: Lead with Compassion

As a changemaker, you'll uncover tough issues that may unsettle your stakeholders. They'll need time to let go of old beliefs before they can act on new insights. Help them manage their discomfort and work together to find a "third way"— a solution that addresses the reality of what you've discovered while considering the complexities of acting on it.

13

Manage Timeline Change Requests

"**W**E NEED TO CUT three weeks from our project timeline." These words are said nonchalantly, as if what's being asked is no big deal. They're also—most often—communicated as a directive, not a suggestion. Leaving you, innovator, feeling cornered and trapped. Soooo fun, right?

I know it seems like there's no way out of this situation, like you're facing an ultimatum that you *must* obey. I understand.

If you're like me, these few words have hijacked your nervous system. You're now operating on high alert. But are you truly as trapped as you feel?

The answer is a definitive no.

This feeling of being trapped is just that—*a feeling*. You are not as cornered as you think. There is more flexibility in the timeline—and the request to shorten it—than you're being led to believe. Yet, to tap into that flexibility, you must use your sense of confinement as a cue to dig deeper with your stakeholders.

Seek to understand what's driving the request to cut your project timeline. Together, you can find ways to meet your stakeholder's needs without compromising the quality of your work.

This feeling of being trapped is just that— *a feeling*. There is more flexibility in the timeline and the request to shorten it.

What It Looks Like

My team and I were supporting a global home fragrance brand to redefine who their ideal consumer was—what motivates them, their core beliefs and values, key challenges they face, etc. They, like so many other brands, had found that the core DNA of their consumer targets had changed post-pandemic. This work was designed to reconnect the team with their brand's role in consumers' lives today.

The project timeline was originally scheduled to be fourteen weeks long, ending on May 6. In week seven, my team and I received an email from our client contact:

> Brianna, the world is ever-changing here, as you know …
>
> The good news first: We are going to be able to kick off a huge global meeting with our work. The bad news: The meeting is on April 22.
>
> Do you have time to chat? We need to deliver results the week of April 15.
>
> I can explain more, but this is an AWESOME opportunity, exactly what we want.

My body revolted when I read this email. "What?!? You want us to cut three weeks out of an already aggressive timeline? We aren't even out of the field yet and I'm leaving for a two-week vacation at the end of the week. OMG, OMG, OMG! I don't even know how to process this." Simultaneously, my teammate, as he read this email, was having a similar reaction. The two of us were *freaking* out!

And then I caught myself.

My heart rate had risen. My mind was racing. I was feeling cornered and backed into a wall. But then I thought, *Hold up,*

Brianna. You've been here before. Let's not get the cart before the horse. Have the follow-up discussion before you let yourself travel into the space of full doom and gloom.

I fired back an email:

I can chat tomorrow morning from 9:30–11:30 am. Please send an invite for the time that works best for you.

In the meantime, I'm trying to assess what we can do to accelerate field time.

Before the call that next morning, I had huddled with my teammates to explore how we could speed up the fieldwork and compress the analysis time for the project. I played out various scenarios around resourcing. What was possible with the team currently staffed on the project? What might be possible if I added people to the project?

Based on that exercise, I had a good understanding of the tasks and processes I *could* potentially accelerate—and by how much. But, regardless of which levers I pulled, none of them resulted in the three weeks of reduced timeline desired by my client.

The next morning, my client and I got on the phone. As I listened with an open heart, I learned that the organization was recommitting to a unified global presence for this brand, and our work was a key ingredient in that positioning. In the words of my client, this was, indeed, an *awesome* opportunity that we didn't want to lose. However, I knew that cutting three weeks out of the project schedule wasn't feasible. I had to find the both/and solution here, so I dove in with more questions: "Tell me more. What's driving this recommitment to a global presence for this brand? What's the intended outcome of this specific global meeting?"

My client shared more details, and it became clear that she didn't need the full deliverable for this meeting. She needed insight on the new consumer and how they differed from the pre-pandemic consumer target. She also needed to understand the brand's role in this consumer's life. However, she didn't need—at least for this upcoming meeting—insight into each SKU of the brand. It would be OK if this information was still "in process." Their goal for that meeting was more about providing a point of view to spark provocative discussion. They weren't planning on making any major decisions on the consumer target for the brand in that meeting.

Armed with more context, I clearly saw that we weren't actually talking about accelerating the *full* project by three weeks. We were talking about accelerating only a third of the project's analyses. Feelings of expansion started to flood my body. I could see a way to feasibly make this happen—hallelujah! However, we still needed to find some compromise to support the fast-tracking of those initial analyses.

Typically, we present deliverables to clients in two steps: first to direct stakeholders and then to their broader team. However, the accelerated timeline meant we couldn't follow this process. If we were to meet the deadline for the global meeting, my client wouldn't be able to preview the content before we shared it with her full stakeholder team. Fortunately, she was fine with this. After over a decade of working together, she trusted my team and our work. Given the circumstances, she was comfortable relinquishing this level of control.

As our conversation progressed, she and I explored various scenarios for how to meet her needs while protecting the integrity of the project output. The fieldwork for the project wasn't unfolding as smoothly as we had hoped. I had reservations about our ability to deliver all the fast-tracked analyses she was hoping for.

I was honest about the challenges we were facing and together we brainstormed ways to "close the gap." By the end of the call, I had committed to delivering a portion of the outputs she wanted. How to deal with the others was an open question yet. We decided to wait a few more days to see how the fielding schedule would pan out before making further commitments.

In the end, we were able to fast-track all the analyses that my client needed for her global meeting, helping her and her team to seize this opportunity for greater influence in the organization. We then proceeded onward to complete the other analyses in the timeline we had originally specified for the project. The way the reporting unfolded for that project was unconventional and a bit iterative, but it worked. But it only worked because I used that freak-out moment as an opportunity to dig deeper with my client.

Your Challenge: Resist the Time Tempest

First, take a deep breath. I know you've got lots of emotions swirling within you at this moment. In addition to your nervous system being on edge, you're worried about how this request will impact your ability to deliver the quality work that you've promised. You want to be a good partner to your stakeholder, but if you're being honest, you're not feeling that love right now. You might even feel a bit resentful. I get you. I've been where you are so many times.

But here's what I know to be true: When it comes to timeline change requests, *time* is often not the issue that needs your attention. Adjusting your project timeline is the *answer* that your stakeholder has to another problem they need to solve.

So, what does this mean for you, innovator? Your way out of this anxiety-inducing moment is through a greater understanding of the *root* problem that your stakeholder is trying to address with this "simple" timeline shift.

There are lots of reasons why your stakeholder might be asking for you to speed up a timeline. For instance, maybe some of your stakeholder's hard deadlines have shifted: the date of a board meeting, a product launch date, a new important meeting on the horizon, etc. Maybe your key stakeholder is just fearful of losing their peer engagement along the project journey. All of these motivators (and many others not listed) give reason to the request for speeding up a project timeline. And all of these are completely valid. However, the answer for addressing these concerns doesn't always have to be a shortened timeline. Let me explain.

If the board meeting date has been moved up, the meeting planners will need the presentation materials earlier than expected. Typically, materials are required one to four weeks in advance. For your timeline, consider negotiating to submit a draft first, with the final version of the materials delivered in the days leading up to the board meeting.

If a new key meeting is scheduled, make sure to understand how your work is intended to influence the discussion of that meeting. Perhaps not everything needs to be fully completed by then. Interim deliverables might just as easily meet stakeholder needs.

If your key stakeholders are fearful of losing the engagement of their peers, maybe the solution is to add additional touchpoints and iterative debrief sessions into the project calendar, not simply speed up the production of the end product.

You get the idea. The words "we need to reduce the timeline of our project" aren't as simple as they seem. Instead of sending you into panic or defensive mode, they should trigger you to respond with "Tell me more. What's happening and why do you feel we need to reduce the timeline of the project?"

As your stakeholder responds, listen closely to both their explicit and implicit needs being shared. Then, collaboratively explore scenarios with your stakeholders on how to meet these needs while maintaining the integrity of your work and preserving your team's energy.

Also know, innovator, that in this situation, you're empowered to ask for what *you need* in return from your stakeholders to accelerate the timeline in question. Do you need them to approve interim deliverables faster? Do you need them to approve work plan adjustments (in terms of resourcing, budget, etc.) to make the ask for an accelerated timeline more feasible?

As you engage in these scenario-planning discussions, keep these last few words of advice front and center:

- Reject scenarios that stir resentment. You'll feel this in your body—an increased heart rate, tightness, or a feeling of being constrained.

- Explore scenarios that create expansion. You'll notice this as a sense of lightness, as if what's being asked of you is truly possible.

- Decline commitments you know you can't deliver. Saying yes when you shouldn't will only damage trust with your stakeholders.

- Clarify the tradeoffs your stakeholders are making when they request a faster project timeline.

Accepting the Challenge: Find the Both/And

Remember, innovator, a request for a shorter timeline is often your stakeholder's solution to another problem. When you feel yourself constrained by timeline change requests, lean into this three-step process, in search of the both/and solution.

Reject scenarios
that stir resentment.
Explore scenarios
that create expansion.
You'll notice this as
a sense of lightness.

Step 1: Gather the facts

Innovator, you're going to do this step *before* you engage your stakeholders in conversation. Your "in-the-moment" nimbleness in that conversation depends on it. So, do the fifteen to twenty minutes of pre-work. Consider the following:

- Where could you tighten up your project timeline without compromise?

- What compromises—by you or your stakeholders—could help further shorten the project timeline?

- What feels nonnegotiable, where compromises or acceleration (on timeline or deliverables) would negatively impact the outcome of your work?

At this stage, you're gaining awareness of the nuances of your timeline, so that you can engage in this scenario-planning exercise with greater confidence and authority. This isn't about firmly committing to anything at this point.

Step 2: Uncover what your stakeholders are aiming to accomplish

Now it's time to engage in direct conversation with your stakeholders.

Why is a timeline reduction, from their perspective, the obvious solution to their problem? To open this conversation, start with a straightforward prompt: "Tell me more. What's happening and why do you feel we need to reduce the timeline of the project?"

Then, just let them talk. As you listen, jot down everything your stakeholders stand to gain by shortening your project timeline.

Step 3: Engage in scenario planning
to define the both/and solution

Your challenge is to create at least three different ways you can either meet your stakeholders' needs or get closer to them (compared to the current timeline). I've found it effective to do this scenario planning live with your stakeholders, talking it out. That dialogue looks something like this:

> I first want to confirm that I understand your main concern. You're looking to present a well-informed perspective on how the post-pandemic consumer views the brand and its role in their life. You believe having this insight will boost your team's credibility and influence at the global meeting, right?

Let your stakeholder confirm or correct your understanding of their needs. Then, state what you believe they need from you to ultimately achieve this goal. For example:

> So, if I'm understanding correctly, you're not asking to accelerate the entire project deliverable by three weeks. Instead, you need specific pieces of data: a clear definition of your new consumer and the role the brand plays in their lives. This focused information will allow you to start your discussions with your global colleagues as planned.

Again, let your stakeholder confirm or correct your understanding of the goal.

Once you've aligned on needs and goals, you're set to develop a plan on how to proceed.

> Okay, we can definitely deliver the data on who your consumer is by the deadline, as we're already 80 percent through that fieldwork. However, I'm less confident about having the "role of the brand" data for this new consumer target ready, since that fieldwork is progressing slowly. But we do have some viable options.

Option A: We already have substantial insight into the role and significance of the brand for enthusiasts. These people are not necessarily your core consumer target, but analyzing their information would offer a glimpse of what's to come in the full deliverable.

Option B: We could reconsider our recruitment criteria for your core consumer target. Currently, we require qualifying participants to have used the product three times in the last month, and we're losing 10 percent of potential respondents with this criterion. Would lowering the requirement to two uses in the last month work? This adjustment could speed up our data collection.

Option C: Alternatively, we can just focus on producing a detailed analysis of the new consumer target. In this case, we'll do our best to gather the "role of the brand" data as fieldwork progresses, treating it as a "best efforts" part of this interim deliverable, based on how quickly we can gather the necessary information.

Once you've laid out the options, weigh the pros and cons of each scenario with your stakeholder. In the example I just shared, we decided to move forward with Option A. I left the call knowing my team would fast-track the new consumer data cut and the overall role and meaning of the brand data cut—but only for brand enthusiasts, not the new consumer target.

I emerged from this conversation with a plan that felt doable. It was going to require some deviation from Sylver Consulting's typical deliverable production process. However, it's something we could do, and no one was going to lose vacation time or experience sleepless nights to make it happen.

And my client walked away feeling empowered. She and her colleagues were going to have the information they needed to make the most of this unexpected, but extremely fortuitous shift in the global dynamics of the brand. It was a win-win.

But, again, it would not have been that win-win had I stayed in the freak-out space of "OMG! You need us to reduce this timeline by three weeks?!" Using this moment as the trigger to go deeper is what enabled us to get there, and that's exactly what I want you to do when you find yourself in a similar position.

What to Expect

When faced with what seems like an unrealistic timeline request, your instinctive response will be a mix of stress, panic, and perhaps a bit of people-pleasing tinged with resentment. Such requests can throw your thoughts into chaos.

As an innovator, it's crucial for you to train yourself and your team to see this moment of hopelessness as a signal to step back. Use it as a prompt to initiate a deeper dialogue with your key stakeholders and ask more probing questions.

And remember that discussions around reducing project timelines should not be happening via email or through Slack threads. These conversations should always happen live, as the back-and-forth dialogue allows you to fully grasp the nuances of your stakeholders' evolving needs and goals. It also gives you the space to co-create potential solutions and then discuss their implications in real time.

During these conversations, pay attention to your body's response; it will signal when you've arrived at a feasible solution. Your body will feel more expanded. What felt impossible as you stepped into this conversation will start to feel doable. You'll start to breathe a bit easier, and your brain's frenzied activity will calm.

It's important that you emerge from this conversation not feeling resentful of what your stakeholders are asking of you, and it's equally important to protect the quality of the work in whatever compromises are defined. If either of these is at risk, then you have a responsibility to push back on the timeline change request. Your stakeholders might not be thrilled with you initially, but in my experience, they'll understand and come around eventually.

Mindset Shift: **Resist the Time Tempest**

Your stakeholder sees adjusting your project timeline as a way to solve a problem they're facing. However, shortening the timeline is usually just one of several possible solutions to address their needs. Knowing this, resist the urge to panic. Instead, approach the request with curiosity by asking, "Tell me more." This approach helps you explore both/and solutions—pathways forward that meet the needs of your stakeholders without sacrificing the quality of your work or your own personal boundaries.

14

Pause When Leadership
Shifts Occur

A S AN EXTERNAL CONSULTANT, I find that announcements regarding changes of project ownership often come to me via email. And nearly every one of these emails downplays the impact that a change in leadership implies for the project itself.

The tone of these emails tends to be stoic and matter of fact: "I wanted to give you a heads up ... so and so is no longer going to be managing the project." If someone is appointed to step into that role, they let me know who that person is. If someone has not yet been appointed, they might convey a general plan forward ... or not. Nearly every "change of leadership" communication ends with the same sum-up statement: "You should proceed forward as previously defined."

But I'm here to tell you, innovator: The request for you to "proceed forward as previously defined" is a delusion. Yes, it communicates what your broader stakeholders hope can happen, but more times than not, it's a false hope. "Proceeding forward as previously defined" is an order that you should outright disobey. Charging forward as if nothing has changed will only get you into hot water.

Instead, the right response is to pause, to take the time to re-ground all parties engaged in the project, before proceeding at all. Why? Because these shifts inevitably disrupt the ecosystem in which you're executing your work. This doesn't mean your project is doomed. But it does mean you should take the time to acknowledge that these changes could influence your initiative—positively or negatively.

What It Looks Like

This case study is a bit different from others I've shared throughout the book. In this instance, I'm going to show you what happens when you *don't* heed the warning to pause for a regroup in light of a leadership shift. First, let me set some up-front context.

This project—designed to create innovative solutions to address homelessness—was approved in February 2023. I was hired to coach a group of city and community leaders through the innovation process. The goal of the project was to create a portfolio of solutions that, if implemented together, would reduce the scale of homelessness being experienced in the community.

The first task involved identifying which city and community members to include in the project team. Two teams were being staffed: a core team that would work on the project day-to-day and an auxiliary team that would play an advisory role throughout the initiative. It took four months to identify the twenty-six team positions that we had to fill—three months longer than anticipated!

Meanwhile, the homelessness challenge in this community was escalating. The number of people experiencing homelessness had increased and the community was becoming more divided on how to approach this challenge. To say the heat had been turned up would be an understatement. Everyone wanted a solution, and the community felt it was crucial to have this solution sooner rather than later. What's more, there was a growing consensus in the community that the city needed a low-barrier shelter to curb the upward trend of homelessness in the region.

My project leader, the city manager at that time, reached out to say, "Brianna, how can we get to a solution sooner than eight months from now?"

After a number of conversations, we decided to move away from the original scope of work (which included a research discovery phase) and move toward a Test-and-Learn Approach, where we'd use the project budget to shape the community's expression of a low-barrier shelter (remember chapter 2 where I challenged you to meet your stakeholders where they were and embrace a Test-and-Learn Approach? This is a situation where I did that).

Finally, in June 2023, we were ready to kick off the project. *Hallelujah!* I thought. We had our new charge, a team (finally!), and a kickoff workshop on the calendar. Then—four days before that kickoff workshop—I got an email letting me know (matter-of-factly, of course) that the city manager had taken an immediate leave of absence from the city. All city staff had been told to proceed as if no leadership change had occurred. The message for me: "Stay the course."

I felt uneasy about this plan because I hadn't yet completed the pre-workshop sync with the city manager—it was scheduled for the day after this announcement. While I knew who was on the team, I had no idea what they knew about the initiative, its focus, or the time commitment involved. In short, there were significant communication gaps, and no one was available to fill them in.

Part of me knew we should call off the workshop. At that moment, we had no project owner, and the city was in free fall without their city manager. But I had bought my flight tickets, lunch had been ordered, and all twenty-six leaders had cleared their calendars for that 1.5-day kickoff workshop (not an easy feat!).

The sunk costs played a big role in my decision to "stay the course" instead of doing what I knew was right at the time: canceling the workshop and allowing things to settle before starting afresh.

I chose to silence the warning bells and charged forth with the workshop as planned. Day 1 of the workshop was OK. There was tension in the room (due to the community division around the homelessness challenge), but there also seemed to be a collective commitment to work through the discomfort. We were moving in the right direction. I felt cautiously optimistic.

But Day 2 was a different story. *Mutiny* might best describe the tone of the room that day. The team pushed back on the pivot toward a Test-and-Learn Approach, frustrated that a low-barrier shelter solution was being pursued without up-front discovery research. Adding to the tension, the community's distrust of the previous city manager (who had hired me) extended to me, even though I didn't fully understand why at the time.

It was a *hot mess*, if there ever was one! And it was destructive. In the days following that work session, the local media ran my name through the mud, spouting not-nice things about me, most of which didn't have a kernel of truth to them. My body was breaking under the stress of the situation, with weird health issues popping up left and right. (Remember that incredibly stressful project that I mentioned back in the "On the Runway" chapter? This is that one!)

The project suffered as well. We ultimately had to pause the initiative for another three months before everyone could get aligned on how to move forward. Now that original eight-month timeline had become fourteen!

In the end, we got through that project and achieved a superb result. New leadership decided to pivot back to the original project design—the work plan that included the up-front discovery research. A portfolio of nine solutions emerged from the initiative; a low-barrier shelter was only one of those nine solutions. Perhaps, most importantly, the community was now aligned and working together toward the shared goal of reducing homelessness. No longer were leaders working at odds with one another.

But, friends, we definitely could have gotten to this superb result through a much less tumultuous path, had I chosen to push back on the directive to stay the course. I should have taken the moment to say, "Hold up. We need to pause and discuss the implications of this leadership shift." Because you know what? Nothing "stayed the course" with that leadership shift . . . absolutely nothing!

We moved away from the Test-and-Learn Approach and back to the full-discovery approach. We had to develop a whole new engagement plan for city leadership, as the new interim city manager was not on the core team of the project. Ultimately, I had to assume more responsibility than anticipated in keeping the new city manager and the governing body informed of project developments. Additionally, the full project schedule was extended by nearly seven months (between this pause and the time it took to get the first project team established), effectively doubling the resource allocation commitment for the project from my end.

But "stay the course"!

By now, I hope you have a new level of appreciation for my earlier comment that the directive to "proceed forward as previously defined" in a situation like this is a fantasy, a false hope, a lofty and unreasonable aspiration. When you hear these

When a leadership shift occurs, a project's ecosystem changes. Sometimes these changes are minor and other times, major.

words, I encourage you *not* to act on them. Rather, I suggest you use these words as the cue to bring everyone together for an implications conversation.

Your Challenge: Resist the Urge to Plow Ahead

If you fall victim to people-pleasing tendencies, like I do, you're going to want to be a good partner and do as you're told. You're going to be naive and believe that the person telling you to forge ahead (as though nothing has changed) knows something that you don't, that they're wise to other contextual details that make that path feasible.

And you're going to *want* to believe them. Things are so much easier if everything truly does stay the same. But it so rarely does.

Once you start discussing how the leadership change affects your project, expect some parameters to shift. Some changes might be small, impacting only how the work is done, while others could be significant, requiring adjustments to the scope, budget, timeline, and more.

You certainly didn't sign up for any of this! But here you are, nevertheless. And so, your challenge, dear innovator, is to deal with it head on, to advocate for a pump of the brakes to address all the potential ripples (or waves!) this nonchalant communication implies, even if (and I'd argue *especially* if) others engaged in the project are championing a "stay the course" strategy.

Continuing to plow ahead—without taking that moment to regroup—can leave your project blemished forevermore. Best-case scenario, the project outputs are deemed OK, maybe not fully on point, but in the zone. Worst-case scenario, feelings of distrust will emerge that cause blockers and barriers around every turn. As you can see, even the "best-case scenario" feels less than ideal.

While you can do major damage to your project by pushing onward, the cost of demanding a momentary pause is fairly benign. It's possible that the people informing you of this leadership shift might be annoyed or frustrated that you're pushing back. But this momentary discomfort will pass; everyone will move on, and your project will be set up for greater success as a result.

Accept the Challenge: Assess the Ecosystem Impact

As we've established, when a leadership shift occurs, a project's ecosystem changes. Sometimes these changes are minor and other times, major. Bottom line: when a leadership shift is first announced, you simply don't know the full implications of that change. It best serves the project, then, to bring people together to reflect on how this leadership change might impact your project's next steps.

When engaging in this assessment, consider factors such as the following:

Project vision: How might the project's vision and priorities shift under new leadership?

Team dynamics: What changes in team roles and structure might be necessary to align with new leadership?

Communication: How do new leaders prefer to communicate, and what might be required to meet these preferences?

Timeline: How might the leadership change impact key milestones on your project timeline? What strategies will you use to address or mitigate these delays?

Resource: Who will be responsible for bringing new leaders up to speed, and how much time will it effectively require?

Risk identification: What new risks does the leadership shift introduce to your project? Which previous risks might it alleviate or eliminate?

Stakeholder engagement strategy: What adjustments might be required of your stakeholder engagement plans, to reflect the new leader's level of influence and trust with key stakeholders?

Had I done this right with the homeless initiative, I would have canceled the kickoff workshop—it was too soon after the announcement of such a major leadership change. Once the timing was right, I would have involved the new city manager in a conversation about the project.

I would have approached that conversation ready to share the current project scope, explaining how it had shifted under the former city manager and the reasons behind those decisions. I would have asked openly and without judgment whether continuing with this vision and strategy felt right or if pivoting back to the original scope was a better option.

I would have clarified the team's roles and responsibilities and set expectations for communication and stakeholder engagement. I would have outlined the risks I foresaw with the leadership change and invited their input on potential challenges.

Finally, I would have addressed any anticipated changes to timelines or resources based on the next steps we agreed upon. In short, I would have taken a step-by-step look at every aspect of the project and how this leadership shift could impact it.

As it was, I did have this conversation, but ended up having it televised with the governing body instead of just with the city manager. (I wouldn't wish that experience on anyone. It felt like I was being interrogated.) However, regardless of the discomfort, the outcome of that connection was successful, and it got us back on track with the project.

As you do step into these conversations in the future, I urge you to do so unattached to the outcome. All that you previously planned has effectively been thrown out the window, whether you've come to that realization yet or not. This is a moment of re-grounding for you, your project, and your project team. It's best to simply lay out all the project details, using those eco-system components as a guide, and then, when you're done, invite open dialogue with these two questions:

1 What are you hearing that resonates?
2 What concerns or questions do you have?

Listen closely to the answers, as they will reveal the necessary adjustments to get your project back on track.

What to Expect

Losing a project owner often feels like an unnecessary and frustrating setback. You know that you need to pause for this conversation. Yet, you don't really want to. This often leads to delays, extra work, rework, and sometimes changes in goals or deliverables. Even though you didn't make the decision for someone to leave (or be let go), you're the one left to handle the ripple effects.

At first, you're going to want to deny the reality of your situation, that aspects of your project will need to shift to accommodate the changes that have occurred with its leadership. You might feel tempted to "carry on as if nothing has changed," especially if that's the message coming through in emails. Essentially, you're being given permission to pretend everything is fine.

Instead, I want you to do what you know is the right and responsible thing and bring all the key players together for a re-grounding conversation. You might get some initial push-back on this, as people may legitimately not have time for this conversation, given the leadership shifts. Be respectful of and patient with the space people need to get recentered before reengaging with your project.

However, let them know that a conversation is needed before moving forward with the next steps in the project timeline. Be clear and firm about setting this expectation, explaining why it's essential for the project's success. When the conversation happens, come prepared with materials to bring everyone up to speed. Approach the discussion with an open mind and heart, staying flexible and unattached to any specific outcome.

Think of this conversation as a Setting the Stage for Success workshop happening mid-project. By taking the time to have this discussion and helping the new project leader fully embrace the initiative's vision and goals, you'll build greater alignment, engagement, and collaboration around your work. This stronger partnership will set the foundation for a successful outcome.

Mindset Shift: Resist the Urge to Plow Ahead

Leadership changes will impact your project—it's only a question of how. Instead of just following a "stay the course" directive, take the initiative to bring new leaders into a conversation. Together, assess how the recent changes might affect your project and its intended outcomes.

PART THREE

Safe

Landing

"Leaders become great, not because of their power, but because of their ability to empower others."

JOHN C. MAXWELL

THIS BOOK HAS, thus far, been about the creation part of the innovation process. We've discussed what your pre-jump preparations should include to best set your project up for success; we've navigated what it looks like to take the leap into project execution; and we've considered how to maneuver the project mid-flight, making ongoing adjustments as needed to keep your project on track. This next and final section of the book is all about helping you "stick the landing" of your project, ultimately ensuring that what you've created graduates into implementation and that the teams responsible for execution have all that they need to do so successfully.

You'll notice this section is much shorter than the previous ones. That's because if you've done your homework up front—especially with the practices from Part 1—sticking the landing isn't hard. Your project has been aligned with the organization's needs all along, so implementation is imminent.

Yet, the actual landing can be smooth or bumpy. I want it to be smooth for you, dear innovator. To ensure that your new innovation and insights get actioned as intended, we have to back up to the moment when you choose to deploy your parachute and begin to navigate your descent. This is the moment in the innovation journey when you seek to gain commitment (not interest) for implementation from organizational stakeholders and partners. It's the moment when you first begin to share the control of *what has been created* with others, eventually transferring the responsibility of its execution and ownership to others completely.

There can be a tendency, at this wrap-up stage in an innovation process, for a touch of "senioritis" to take root. Your work as the innovator and creator is fast coming to a close. You might be getting itchy for your next challenge, tiring of the one in front of you. I feel you. I've been there—many times over—but I urge you to stay focused and disciplined. Innovations don't see the light of day without good implementation teams. And you have an important handoff role to play yet. So, let's get to work on reviewing what you can personally do to navigate your project to an uncomplicated and comfortable landing.

15

Empower Implementation Partners

YOUR JOB AS AN INNOVATOR is to birth ideas. And while these ideas may be amazing, inspiring, and purposeful, they won't activate on their own. No, you need someone to commit to growing your idea, someone who will adopt and nurture it, someone who will ensure that it grows to its fullest potential.

In an ideal world, your implementation partners have been traveling the path of innovation with you, plugging in at key points along the way. If this is true, they understand what you're striving to accomplish and why they've been tapped as the implementation partner for the initiative. Likely, they've also been engaged, on some level, in co-creating the emerging solution. Maybe they participated in the ideation sessions that prompted the idea-in-discussion or maybe they've been a voice of expertise as you've shaped that idea for maximum impact.

Regardless of how your stakeholders have been engaged to date, what you need to understand is that engagement doesn't equal commitment to implementation. Yes—stakeholder engagement is, indeed, an important indicator of success, as it demonstrates interest in and curiosity about the innovation taking shape. However, engagement in *your* innovation process does not guarantee that your implementation partners are now willing to lead the execution of that same idea and be held accountable for its success.

You're essentially looking for someone to adopt your child (your idea), and they may feel like their "house" is a bit too full already—they've already got too much on their plate. Your implementation partners need to feel connected to your idea; they need to see how it aligns to their goals and priorities for the organization before you're likely to get that emphatic "Yes!" for implementation support. This is where I suggest you lean in, innovator. Help your implementation partners consciously assess if and when this new initiative should get their focus.

What It Looks Like

This project focused on tools and platforms to help small and medium-sized businesses (SMBs) manage online stores, including shipping, inventory, and customer service integration. While the market insights team hired Sylver Consulting, it was the UX team's job to implement the solutions we developed.

The UX team had been involved in the project all the way through and were genuinely excited about the solutions that emerged. Yet here we were at the end of the project, with a looming question: *What comes next?*

We supported this team to answer that question by conducting what we call a Go Forward Workshop. This workshop is designed to evaluate the merit of moving new initiatives forward (compared to other priorities in a team's product roadmap). If proceeding is deemed beneficial, then tactical steps required to move each solution forward are defined.

In the case of this project, the Go Forward Workshop was a day-long event consisting of four activities.

First, we conducted an ALUO assessment of three potential new solutions. To support that assessment, we asked four key questions:

1 **Advantages:** In what ways does this solution support the team to meet the three core goals of the initiative? (We had come to use "divert" and "convert" as shorthand for two of the goals, each about changing how SMBs approach their online sales. The third goal was called "leapfrog" and spoke to the intent to lead the industry in digital retail tools for SMBs).

2 **Limitations:** Are there concerns or watchouts to be mindful of? In what ways might this solution work against the three core goals of the initiative?

3 **Unique Qualities:** What about this solution is unique compared to others under development or in consideration? What about this solution is unique compared to the competition?

4 **Overcome Limitations:** What would it take for the organization to overcome the expressed concerns or watchouts?

After this assessment, the team decided that only two of the three solutions were worth implementation focus. Now, we needed to define what "moving forward" tangibly looked like for each.

We broke the two solutions into detailed features—nine for one and fifteen for the other—and then mapped each feature onto a graph. The y-axis showed each feature's potential to change online selling behavior (convert/divert), while the x-axis measured how unique that feature was compared to competitors in the e-commerce industry.

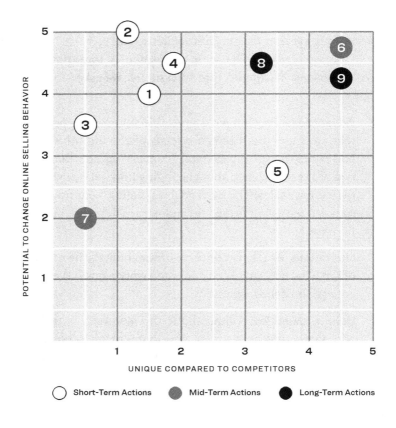

Each number on the graph represented a solution feature, visually showing how it aligned with leadership goals. For example, #1 represented automating address validation at checkout to improve accuracy and reduce frustration, while #2 stood for enabling batch label printing to streamline bulk order processing. You get the idea.

The group reviewed each feature, one at a time. First, we discussed and agreed on its placement on the y-axis, then did the same for the x-axis. We did this exercise on a whiteboard.

After mapping all the features on the graph, we created an execution roadmap for each e-commerce solution. With the features and their impact clearly visualized, it was easy for the team to prioritize short-term (within a year), mid-term (next year), and long-term (two or more years) actions for each solution.

At the end of the workshop, the team felt aligned on the role that each solution was going to play toward achieving their leadership goals and the steps and timeline required to get there. This level of specification was concrete and tangible, supporting the UX team in gaining quick development traction. Eight months later, this alignment proved catalytic, culminating in the release of their first product, a testament to the effectiveness of the one-day workshop.

Your Challenge: Be a Facilitator

By default, your innovation will get added to the "list" of your implementation team. However, without a clear, urgent purpose, that idea is unlikely to be prioritized for action.

I'm challenging you to take action and avoid falling into default mode, innovator. Help your implementation partners see how your idea aligns with their goals. Your chances of gaining traction increase if your initiative can be integrated into their current workstream. Knowing this, you certainly have your work cut out for you.

And that work starts sooner than the end of your project. As soon as your implementation partners come into view (which could be at the start of your project or mid-initiative), you need to make it your mission to understand what leadership is holding them accountable for. Then, use those goals as North Star guideposts for your work while continuously looking for points of connection.

The exercises in chapters 4, 5, and 6 highlight what's most important to your team and partners. Ideally, implementation partners were part of these discussions from the start, shaping your project toward a successful outcome. If they weren't involved early on, revisit chapter 4 and guide them through the Five Intention-Setting Questions. This ensures you're aligned on their priorities, especially as they are key to implementing your initiative.

To keep your project aligned with the goals and needs of your implementation partners, have regular check-ins throughout your innovation initiative. Ask what they're learning and how it impacts their team's goals. *Are your innovation outcomes bringing them closer to those goals, or creating new challenges?* These questions will help you course correct as needed as you move through your project.

Yet—even with these iterative conversations happening—there are still risks. The implementation team might still shelve your work and refuse to act on it. This is where we enter into the focus of this challenge.

When possible—and to be clear, it isn't always possible—I encourage you to help your implementation partners assess how your current innovation work stacks up to the other priorities that they are working towards. The goal in doing this is not to push the outcomes of your work to the front of their development roadmap. Rather, it's about taking stock—of where they are and how what you've learned and created through your innovation efforts may (or may not) help them to achieve their goals sooner, more effectively.

It's important that you enter this conversation unattached to the outcome. Your role is that of a facilitator, where you're helping the team critically assess if the path they're heading down is, indeed, the path that they should continue down. Or if they should alter the plan to make space for the new

Help your implementation partners see how your idea aligns with their goals.

short- or long-term innovations that have emerged in your recent initiative.

Sometimes, the answer to this assessment will fast-track your innovation into implementation. Other times, your innovation will still be placed at the end of the development list. The implementation position doesn't matter. Being conscious and intentional about where the team places the new innovation in a development roadmap does.

Now, some implementation partners are going to be happy to engage in this dialogue with you. Others will get territorial. To curb the defensiveness, I recommend you build this step into your project plan from the start. Set expectations from the beginning that this discussion *will* occur. This prewarning will help facilitate buy-in for this broader prioritization step, more than if you spring it on people at the end of your project.

If feasible, request that your implementation partners share their development roadmap prior to this step. While it's not essential to have this roadmap before moving into a Go Forward Workshop, having it can be beneficial. A documented roadmap often means it's been communicated across the organization, providing valuable context about existing expectations that have been set with leadership. These expectations shape what stakeholders will advocate for—and what they won't—regarding your idea.

Accept the Challenge: Facilitate a Go Forward Workshop

First, be aware that not all implementation partners are going to be up for a Go Forward Workshop. And, more than likely, you'll get a lot of pushback on taking a day to execute this workshop.

While you certainly can't *make* your implementation partners participate, I encourage you to continually reinforce the value of this workshop frequently and iteratively throughout your initiative. The output of this workshop acts as a bridge between the idea and its execution; it's the moment in an innovation project when an idea's ownership and accountability transfers from the innovation team to the business/operations teams.

You can conduct this workshop in less than a day, but be aware that reducing the duration may diminish the clarity and detail of the plans that emerge. Each hour cut impacts the depth and practicality of the outcomes.

During this workshop, you play the role of a facilitator. You've guided the team in developing the ideas, and now it's up to your implementation partners to determine how to turn these ideas into reality and take ownership of them.

Four key activities happen to support that transfer of ownership:

Activity 1: Perform an ALUo assessment on the idea (or ideas)

On a whiteboard (or a large Post-it), create a table with four columns. Label each column with one of the following titles:

- Advantages
- Limitations
- Unique Qualities
- overcome limitations

Share the idea with the team. Then, lead them through a reflective discussion, referencing each column of the table. (Look back to the "What It Looks Like" section of this chapter for the specific probing questions to ask for each of the ALUO column headers.)

Once you're at the end of this reflective conversation, ask the team:

- Given the discussion we just had, does it make sense to move forward with this idea?

- What, if anything, do we need to change about the idea to better align it with the team's core goals and objectives?

Activity 2: Delineate the features and capabilities required to make the idea real

On a whiteboard or large Post-it, list all the features and capabilities needed to bring the idea to life. Keep adding them until the team agrees everything important is covered, then number each item.

Activity 3: Map the features and capabilities back to the project goals

This step will vary based on your project and workshop time. In my case study, we used the graph to discuss each feature's role in meeting leadership goals. If time is tight, simplify by asking, "Which leadership goal does this action most support?"

Activity 4: Create the action roadmap

Next, create a three-column table on a whiteboard (or a large Post-it). Label each column as follows:

- Short-Term Actions
- Mid-Term Actions
- Long-Term Actions

Work with your implementation partners to define what constitutes a short-term, mid-term, and long-term action. In the case study I shared, we defined short-term actions as items that would be implemented that year; mid-term actions were punted to the following year; and long-term actions were to be implemented in two or more years.

Now, with your timeline defined, slot each of your features and capabilities into one of those columns. Note: This can be a lengthy conversation, as many actions are interdependent on other activities and the priorities of your implementation team. So, just make sure that you have the space allotted to support this conversation.

What to Expect

As I mentioned above, you can expect pushback on doing a Go Forward Workshop. It's common for implementation partners to say that they don't have time to be part of a session like this. But be persistent. This is an important bridge moment for your project.

When your implementation partners fully participate, they'll leave with less anxiety and a clear action plan. What felt uncertain at first will turn into concrete, actionable steps. Together, you'll transform your vision into practical, scheduled tasks. This process—combining thoughtful planning and a bit of magic—helps bring your ideas to life!

However, it's crucial not to force participation. If the implementation team is genuinely reluctant to engage in this session and you push it through, the results are likely to be ineffective. Your partners might create an implementation plan but will be unmotivated to execute it. In this case, it's better for you to just acknowledge that you've done all that you can and it's time to bless and release this project and your ideas. The next step actions will be taken when the timing is right.

Mindset Shift: Be a Facilitator

Transferring ownership of new ideas to an implementation team requires more than just sparking their interest. The team must see how these ideas align with their leadership goals. As an innovator, you can use your facilitation skills to help them assess the value of each new innovation and create clear, actionable steps for its effective execution.

Create and Sustain Implementation Momentum

THE HARDEST PART of doing anything new is starting. That's because there are *so many* mind games that can stand in the way of taking that first step—for you, your implementation partners, and the organization at large. Factors influencing these mind games include (but are certainly not limited to) the following:

- Change is hard and intimidating. Because of this, we tend to postpone starting anything new for as long as possible.

- No one wants to fail. The easiest way to avoid failure is to never start or try something new. This fear is even stronger in organizational cultures that penalize failure.

- Fear of looking foolish. No one wants to hear "you didn't think this through" after an innovation flops. To avoid this, we keep analyzing, making business cases, and checking with others—always finding one more reason to delay action.

- Insufficient resources can become an excuse. We tell ourselves that we lack money, staff, or approvals to begin.

We convince ourselves that it is safer to wait for more resource-flush days.

* Other priorities take precedence. With busy schedules and never-ending to-do lists, lack of bandwidth becomes an easy, justifiable reason to delay action.

But the thing is, you and your implementation partners have gotten to this point, innovator. Verbal commitments to take action on the innovations created have been made. You've done the assessment to ensure that the new innovations will support you and your team to yield growth goals. And you have a roadmap of next step actions defined.

Now, it's time to JFDI, my friend—just freaking do it. It is time to act!

What It Looks Like

My team was working with a municipality to create a plan for how the city could launch heating and cooling centers across the city. This, on face value, seemed like it should be a fairly simple task. A city has access to lots of facility space. Shouldn't it be easy to open the doors 24/7 to residents who need respite from the extreme heat or cold?

Not so much. It turns out, there are some major barriers to setting up respite centers that never close. Chief among these challenges are staffing, staff training (so they can meet the various physical and mental needs of individuals using the center), sufficient security resources, and coordinated communication and messaging with the broader community.

We convened a cross-functional group of city leaders for a two-phase workshop. In just four hours (on Day 1), we identified eight actionable strategies to tackle challenges in staffing, training, security, and communication. On Day 2, we spent another four hours delineating the team's "Rocks" for the next ninety days. Rocks refer to the top three to seven actions that a team will put focus on—actions that, if accomplished, will yield traction in support of their goal. In this case, the goal was to have heating and cooling centers up and running by winter.

The team went through a three-step process to yield their Rocks of focus.

Step 1: Create a master task list

I tasked the team with generating a comprehensive list of all the major short-term tasks essential for getting the heating and cooling centers up and running by winter. Twenty-two activities were defined—way too many for the seven people in attendance that day. We needed to narrow those short-term priorities into a manageable set—meaning three to seven at max.

Step 2: Define three to seven priorities

Every workshop participant was asked to survey the original twenty-two tasks and to then vote for three to five actions they felt would *best* move the team towards its goal of having the centers established by winter. Every action that received a vote was put into a "keep" bucket.

Those that didn't get votes were thrown into the "kill" bucket (not kill forever, just set aside for the next ninety days).

We found ourselves with thirteen items still in the "keep" bucket—too many to achieve the traction we needed. We methodically went through each item, asking those who voted for a task to explain why it was critical to tackle now. This discussion allowed us to explore possibilities for merging tasks or further sharpening our focus to ensure more effective progress.

At last, we had narrowed it down to eight actions in the "keep" bucket, still one too many. It was time to be ruthless. To achieve the momentum we desired, we needed to be decisive—we could only proceed with three to seven key next steps.

We held another voting round, this time asking everyone to select their top three actions. I posed the question, "Which of these actions will *best* prepare the city to launch a 24/7 heating center by winter?" Four actions emerged as essential.

Step 3: Create SMART goals

We had identified our necessary actions but had not yet outlined how to successfully execute them within the next ninety days, nor had we assigned responsibility for each task. The final step in our Rocks exercise involved setting SMART goals for each action in the "keep" bucket and assigning task owners. SMART goals ensure each objective is as follows:

Specific: The goal is clear and well-defined within the timeline.

Measurable: Progress and completion are quantifiable.

Achievable: The goal is realistic and considers available resources and time.

Relevant: Each goal directly supports our broader project aims.

Time-bound: There is a definitive deadline for completing the task.

At the end of this workshop, the team had four key SMART goals of focus:

1   Two team members (representing HR and the Office of Sustainability) would get at least one of the four major city government players (i.e., mayor, controller, city council, and director of HR) to buy into the new staffing model for a 24/7 heating center in the next ninety days.

2   One member of the team (representing the Office of Sustainability) committed to reviewing all current Community Emergency Response Team (CERT) communications. In

the next ninety days, she would identify opportunities to make CERT material clearer, thus enabling the team to reach out to the community for more volunteers once city leadership had bought into the new staffing model for the initiative.

3 Two additional team members (representing the current CERT program and the police department) would reach out to five or more local organizations to see if they would be willing to support the heating and cooling center initiative, either by offering volunteers to address staffing challenges or by providing supplies like food, cots, blankets, and so on.

4 Two members (representing parks and recreation) would identify the best facility for a 24/7 heating center.

In the end, when this team walked away from this workshop, they knew exactly what they were individually responsible for over the next few months. No *one* person was taking on an enormous amount of work, but every person had a smaller— and *doable*—part to play in the continuation of the project.

Over the course of the following ninety days, the team regrouped once a month to check in on progress and problem-solve issues together. These regular check-ins further supported accountability in the team, prioritizing their Rocks, despite all the other priorities in life demanding their attention.

Ultimately, that team was able to advocate and secure a change in HR policy that made staffing the heating and cooling centers possible. Each member of the team followed through on what they had committed to, and 24/7 heating and cooling centers are now a thing the city just does. It no longer feels like the unachievable, complicated task that it once did. And more, through this process, the team learned how to lean

Organizations fail to gain traction towards their goals because they're trying to do too many things. **The Rocks exercise quiets the noise and focuses execution.**

into cross-departmental collaboration in a whole new way—a skill that has had ripple effects across the city.

Your Challenge: Define Your Rocks

This challenge is a group activity; it's a prioritization technique taught as a core methodology of the Entrepreneurial Operating Systems (EOS) model.

In "Managing Your Rocks," a blogpost on the EOS website, Dean Breyley writes:

> The term "Rock" comes from an analogy in Stephen Covey's book *First Things First*. Picture a glass cylinder set on the table. Next to the cylinder are rocks, gravel, sand and a glass of water. Imagine that the glass cylinder is all the time that you have during a workday. The rocks represent your main priorities and the gravel your day-to-day responsibilities. The sand is interruptions and the water everything else that happens during your day. If you, as most people do, pour the water in first, the sand in second, the gravel in third, and the rocks in last—the rocks won't fit. That's your typical workday.
>
> If you do the reverse and prioritize working on the big stuff first—put the rocks in, next add the gravel, then the sand, and finally pour the water in—everything fits in the glass cylinder perfectly. Therefore, if you work first on your biggest priorities—that is, your Rocks—everything else falls into place.

The Rocks activity is designed to help you and your implementation partners pinpoint and commit to three to seven top priorities, or Rocks, for the next ninety days. When you label a task as a Rock, it means you're dedicating focused effort to it, setting other tasks aside during this period.

Organizations often fail to gain traction towards their goals because they're trying to do too many things, all at once. The Rocks exercise quiets the noise and focuses execution, supporting your team to gain traction and accomplish more. This process breaks the big, overarching vision of your new innovation into achievable, bite-sized chunks.

Accept the Challenge: Determine Your Rocks of Highest Priority

All key project stakeholders need to be engaged in this Rocks exercise. A partial team will not suffice. I recommend that everyone come together for a three-hour work session. This will give you the time and space needed to execute this activity without stress.

At the start of your meeting, guide your team to focus on their current vision. This may involve revisiting the product or offering roadmap that has been steering the team, or it could require refocusing the team on the larger vision of what you're aiming to create. The objective here is to ensure that everyone is in sync and committed to the collective vision you are striving to achieve.

Once everyone is grounded in the vision for your initiative, you're ready to start the Rocks activity. Just like you saw in my story, there are three key steps.

Step 1: Create a master task list

Distribute a stack of Post-it notes to each meeting participant. Pose the question: "Which tasks need attention in the next ninety days for us to achieve the bigger picture goal of our initiative?" Clarify that participants can use as many Post-its as needed, but each should contain just one task. Allow about ten minutes for everyone to jot down their thoughts.

Once everyone is done writing, go around the room and ask each person to share their list. As people share their tasks, post them on a whiteboard or wall at the front of the room. Remove duplicate priorities from the list as you go. For instance, in the case study shared, one person wrote "gain support for the new staffing model from one of the four major city players" as a critical next step, while another person wrote "gain the support of the mayor for the new staffing model." Given that the mayor is one of the major players, we combined these two tasks before continuing to Step 2.

Step 2: Define three to seven priorities

Give each workshop participant five voting dots. Instruct them to survey all the tasks on the board. Then, invite them to vote for the three to five activities they feel are *most* critical to accomplish in the next ninety days. In other words, these priorities, if executed, will tangibly move the team closer to their bigger-picture goal.

Every task that gets a vote—*irrespective of the number of votes*—gets moved to a new area of the whiteboard/wall. This new space represents the "keep" bucket. All other Post-its are retired to a "kill" bucket and discarded as priorities for the next ninety days. (Don't fully trash tasks that go to the "kill" bucket. Just put them aside for now. They may be reconsidered as a priority the next time the team sits down to define their Rocks.)

Within the "keep" bucket, look for additional opportunities to combine tasks. To do this, go around the room and ask each person to share why they voted for the priorities they did.

After merging similar tasks, assess your list. If you have more than seven priorities, it's time for another round of voting, as demonstrated in my story. Encourage decisiveness. For this round, give each participant only three voting dots. Ask them: "Which three tasks are the *most* critical to complete in the next ninety days to support the team's vision?" This helps further narrow down the priorities to the most essential actions.

At this point, you'll likely have three to seven priorities defined. If not, spark another round of dialogue, where people advocate for why they feel certain priorities are more critical than others. Continue this conversation until the group is aligned around the three to seven priorities of focus for the next ninety days.

Step 3: Create SMART goals

Now, transform these priorities into actionable SMART goals: Specific, Measurable, Achievable, Relevant, and Time-bound. For each priority in the "keep" bucket, formulate a SMART goal that

- clearly defines the objective;

- sets measurable outcomes;

- is achievable within the ninety-day timeframe with available resources;

- aligns with the broader vision of the project.

Next, assign an owner to each SMART goal. This person is responsible for driving the goal to completion, though they will likely work with others to achieve it. This step ensures accountability and clear direction for each priority.

Once your SMART goals are set, this Rocks activity is complete. To maintain momentum and ensure progress on these priorities, schedule monthly check-ins lasting thirty minutes to an hour. During these sessions, review steps taken on each team member's Rock(s) and discuss any challenges encountered. Collaboratively problem-solve any obstacles to keep the team on track and moving forward effectively.

Lastly, plan to reconvene your team every ninety days to repeat this Rocks exercise. This regular rhythm ensures the team stays focused and maintains momentum towards implementation—in an aligned and systematic way.

What to Expect

Your role in facilitating Rocks activities, including check-ins and repeated exercises, will vary depending on your position and the organization's structure. As an external consultant, I typically guide teams through their initial Rocks session and then pass the baton to internal teams for subsequent monthly check-ins and workshops. If you're part of an internal innovation team, your implementation partners might benefit from continuous facilitation support, depending on your relationship with them and your team's capacity to provide that ongoing support.

You need to remember, innovator—starting something new is always daunting, as emphasized at the outset of this chapter. The initial ninety-day cycle of the Rocks exercise isn't expected to fully launch your innovation. Rather, it's about establishing a new rhythm and focus around your initiative. This shift helps build momentum and energy within the team—a win that can inspire everyone involved and drive future progress.

When you first introduce the Rocks activity, be prepared for some resistance. This method pushes participants from mere discussion into tangible action, which can be uncomfortable for some. The shift from planning to doing is a big step, and it's natural for this transition to stir up some hesitation or reluctance among team members. Your role as an innovator is to guide your team through these initial challenges.

Despite the initial pushback, the benefits of this exercise are profound. I want to reassure you that the discomfort is temporary, and the outcomes are invariably positive. From my experience, participants always leave the Rocks activity feeling empowered and energized. The process effectively breaks down overwhelming projects into manageable tasks, bringing a sense of clarity and accomplishment that is both rewarding and motivating.

Moreover, the Rocks exercise is especially useful for teams that tend to avoid decisive action. It helps cut through procrastination and encourages a more proactive mindset. Teams emerge from this exercise confident and aligned, making them feel more prepared and prone to act.

Mindset Shift: **Define Your Rocks**

What three to seven actions will significantly advance your idea in the next ninety days? Clearly define your key priorities—your Rocks—and then build accountability into those Rocks by setting SMART goals. This clarity and structure will turbo-boost the implementation efforts of your innovation.

17

Let Go

R EACHING THE END of a project is often accompanied by a whirlwind of emotions. You're standing at the threshold of something you've nurtured, grown, and—in some cases—fought for, and now you face the hardest part: letting go.

In our minds, we want this to be a moment of celebration, a time of quick action. You've done something good, you feel proud of your work, and you believe in the merit of the next steps being recommended. In your mind, when you share this work with leadership, they love it and immediately get behind it.

And yet, that doesn't always happen.

Sometimes your vision and recommendations get executed, just as you've suggested. Yet often—and probably more times than not—your recommendations get half-implemented or, possibly, absolutely *nothing* happens.

Often, we gauge our value—and our organization's view of us—by whether our work gets executed. If leadership backs your recommendations and funds your projects, it feels like proof of your worth and success.

So, what happens if your recommendations aren't acted on? Does that mean that you've failed or that your department lacks value?

Not at all. Just because your recommendations aren't immediately put into action doesn't mean that you—or your department—are any less valuable. Sometimes, timing and organizational readiness play a larger role than the quality of your ideas. Your work still adds value by planting seeds for future impact.

In these moments, your mind may fixate on what wasn't done, tempting you into a cycle of rumination. *Why am I even here? They don't trust me, don't appreciate the blood and sweat that I have poured into this work. Do I matter to this organization? Does it even make sense for me to invest as much as I do? Maybe I shouldn't care as much as I do . . .*

But here is the thing, innovator: Change takes time, and it *always* takes longer than we want it to. So, when you limit your perspective to just *the project*—even if it was a smashing success—you are shortchanging the value that you and your team have to offer. In this chapter, I'm telling you: *Stop anchoring yourself purely in the short-term and direct-outcome results of your projects!*

What It Looks Like

In 2022, we partnered with a medical device manufacturer with a clear goal: to "own" the senior living and elder care technology space. Our mission was to identify additional product areas, beyond my client's current safety and emergency response offerings, that could strengthen their brand's association within this domain.

A four-phased process guided the work:

Phase 1: Qualitative research
We conducted interviews with key stakeholders, including seniors, family caregivers, facility staff of senior communities,

Change takes time, and it *always* takes longer than we want it to.

and geriatric healthcare providers to understand their needs, challenges, and expectations in senior living and elder care technology.

Phase 2: Where to Play workshop
We facilitated a four-hour workshop to identify potential portfolio expansion opportunities for our client in the senior living and elder care market.

Phase 3: Market-sizing analysis
We conducted secondary research on six prioritized product expansion categories to assess the market landscape and estimate the "size of prize" opportunity for each.

Phase 4: Ideation workshop
We led an eight-hour Translating Insights into Opportunity workshop, guiding the client team to develop a portfolio of six to eight product ideas aimed at establishing a stronger and broader presence in the senior living and elder care technology market.

We concluded the project with a clear vision for how my client could lead in the senior living and elder care technology space. All the key stakeholders were fully committed to the vision and prepared to drive its next steps, leaving us all feeling accomplished and optimistic.

Yet, three months after wrapping the project, I checked in with the client. No action had been taken on any of our recommendations. The same was true at the six- and nine-month check-ins. It was disheartening. A dozen people had poured their energy into this work for six months. We did everything right—engaged the right people, had regular check-ins with leadership, involved the business in defining the product roadmap—yet it had all been seemingly shelved.

The client claimed they wanted to "own" the senior living and elder care technology market, but I couldn't help my snarky inner voice saying, *Really?! You've been handed the blueprint, and yet ... nothing is happening.*

I'll admit, I had given up hope. Nearly a year after the project wrapped, it seemed like nothing had moved forward. In my mind, I'd already written off this project as a missed opportunity, feeling the blow to my pride (and ego) in the process.

Then, at my one-year check-in with the client, everything shifted. I learned they were exploring an acquisition that would transform their approach to market expansion—fast-tracking their goal of becoming a "formidable player" in record time.

And then, a year after that—now two years post-project—I learned that the acquisition had gone through, and the company had hired a portfolio manager specifically for senior living and elder care technology. This was a game-changer; they'd never had a dedicated resource for this category before!

I also discovered that the work we had done was now a key resource guiding the product pipeline for the newly formed division. While the specific product ideas from our Translating Insights into Opportunity workshop weren't necessarily moving forward—since the acquisition introduced new capabilities— the foundational insights and direction from our overall project had become the North Star for the team now overseeing the senior living and elder care technology portfolio.

In other words, our work was shaping an entirely new business division for the organization. It felt like a phoenix was rising! And here's the thing, innovator ... I would have missed all these incredible updates if I had let the negative talk track take over. Nine months after the project ended, it looked like all our efforts had gone to waste. But that wasn't the case. The business simply needed time to mobilize around the vision that had been created.

Your Challenge:
Surrender the How and When of the Vision

"Most people overestimate what they can do in a year and underestimate what they can do in ten years." This quote—attributed to Bill Gates—plays on repeat in my mind. It serves as a gentle reminder for me to practice patience and extend grace when it comes to project activation.

Yes—our job as innovators is to "push the envelope," "challenge the status quo," and "think outside of the box." That is how we serve the organizations that we support. But, in the end, we're responsible for leading people and organizations through change. And change has a timeline of its own that we just can't control—despite how hard we try.

We often make the mistake of thinking that the big challenge and responsibility of our work is *the project* that we're working on ... the specific "wicked" problem that we're trying to figure out or the "big, hairy, audacious goal (BHAG)" that we're being tasked to achieve. It's not. It's leading the people—and the organization—that we are working with to the call for change.

When people don't immediately act on next steps, we often think we've missed the mark—that we didn't communicate the project's value effectively or make a strong enough business case for the recommended next steps. So, what do we do? We double down. We seek more sponsorship, find new ways to present the project, and constantly tweak the business case to justify the vision being presented. In other words, we lean more into responsibility than closure.

The challenge that you are being called to embrace at this stage of your project, innovator, is one of surrender. You've done *everything* that you can to ready the organization and your stakeholders for the change that will help them achieve the desired outcome of your work. And now it is time to let go.

Think of your recommendations as seeds planted deeply in fertile ground. These seeds embody a vision of what a fully grown plant could look like and how it might benefit its surroundings. As the nurturer of that plant, you can't force it to grow faster than the environment allows. Extra water or sunlight won't make it sprout sooner—in fact, it could do more harm than good. It needs time to mature, develop roots, and grow at its own pace.

It is the same with your project recommendations, innovator. You can't rush your stakeholders to act faster than the organization's natural pace.

Accept the Challenge: Balance Your Energy and Expectations

You've done what you were called to do. Take a moment to really sit with that truth.

If you have followed the advice in the pages of this book and have gotten your teams and stakeholders to the outcomes that you promised for your project, you have done your job—and you've done it well.

You should not define your personal worth by what happens next. However, you also shouldn't just throw your hands up and say, "See ya!"

This is the moment in your project when it's time to take a step back energetically and actively seek balance—of both your personal energy and the expectations of those around you.

From a personal energy perspective, it can be frustrating when immediate action is not taken towards the recommendations presented in your work. It's even more devastating and demoralizing when there is an outright "no" received for those recommendations.

However, as my story shows, inaction today does not mean inaction forever. Sometimes, groups and companies just need time to mobilize around and adjust to a new vision. This is about you becoming more compassionate towards your stakeholders and giving space for the seeds that you've planted to germinate.

You'll want to stay "in the project" just enough to check in periodically and see if the seeds you've planted are taking root. But it's just as important to stay "out of the project" enough to strike the right balance—it's time to let other team members or departments take the lead. It's also important to not push your involvement where it might feel like an overreach. This approach allows the team to fully embrace the vision, while you remain a steady but unobtrusive source of support, ensuring you don't take on responsibility where it's neither desired nor beneficial.

For your periodic check-ins, try these three guiding questions:

1   What new actions or decisions have been made because of the project?

2   Have there been any roadblocks in acting on the project results?

3   What unexpected benefits or opportunities have emerged from this work?

Why these three questions? They provide a holistic view of your project's impact.

Question 1 shows the direct impact of your project on the business. Question 2 highlights areas where you might still support the organization in moving toward the vision. Question 3 captures unintended outcomes, giving a complete picture of the project's influence and impact.

What to Expect

As you reach this point in a project's lifecycle—the point of letting go—it's natural to feel the weight of decisions that may diverge from your original vision. You might also experience a sense of frustration or even feeling unappreciated if actions towards recommendations appear stalled. This initial blow can sting, especially when you've invested so much of yourself. But this is a moment to pause, recalibrate, and remind yourself of the larger picture.

Innovation isn't about immediate validation; it's about planting ideas that can influence, inspire, and impact in ways that may only become clear over time. When you stay too focused on the present outcome, you risk becoming shortsighted, reducing the broader impact of your work to a series of tasks rather than a meaningful legacy.

Remember, growth isn't linear. Some projects take years to blossom, while others spark new directions that weren't visible before.

When you're at this point of "letting go," you want to avoid becoming adversarial or overly attached to the specifics of implementation. Instead, lean into the role of a trusted advisor. Rather than burn bridges or let short-term frustrations undermine your broader purpose, aim to support the team and the project in a way that keeps doors open. Trust that the seeds that you have planted are strong enough to grow, even if you're not there to see every step of their journey. Releasing that need for control frees you from unnecessary burdens and allows you to maintain a spirit of openness and possibility. It gives you the energy now to start planting other seeds in other places ... which is exactly what you are meant to do.

Mindset Shift: Surrender the How and When of the Vision

Trust the seeds that you've planted in the work that you've done and give them space to grow—on the timeline that their surroundings support and in ways you might not even expect. Know that you've done your part and that, sometimes, the most powerful—and helpful—thing you can do is to step back and watch what unfolds.

Earn Your Wings

OUR JOURNEY together has come to a close, innovator... at least for now. Yet, I pray that this moment is just the start of your own journey.

You've learned, through this book, what it looks like to *love people* through the innovation process—to meet them where they are. And the truth is sometimes it's easy to show that love to the people you're working with, and other times, you have to *really* work at it ... and it can be hard.

You've witnessed—through my stories—what it looks like to be committed to the flourishing of people. I've shown you what it looks like to be that Care Bear of love, dedicated to helping each person and organization that you serve rise up to be the best version of themselves.

I've illustrated what it looks like to *action love in business*, my friend. And now I'm challenging you to be the winds of change, helping to multiply this impact.

My Invitation: Spread Light

Today's world is saturated with negative emotions, such as fear, anger, envy, greed, and despair. From media broadcasts to corporate cultures to social interactions in our communities,

You must *choose* to be that catalyst of change, innovator. It won't happen if you accept the status quo.

we're often encouraged not only to engage with these emotions but to spread them within our circles. This cycle ultimately fosters division and hate.

But you, innovator, can choose a different path: You can choose to intentionally spread light.

I challenge you to boldly and courageously push back on the negative dynamics that threaten to undermine your innovation projects. Each of the seventeen challenges in this book shows you how to shine light on anxieties, misalignments, doubts, and fear surrounding your innovation work. You're offered tools that, if executed with love, will tangibly impact the quality of your work, improving organizational culture, enhancing employee morale, boosting creativity, and creating more effective team collaboration and so much more.

But you must *choose* to be that catalyst of change, innovator. It won't happen if you accept the status quo.

Your path is likely to be bumpy. At some point (likely many points), you will lose your way. You will find yourself in the thick of difficult moments. Narratives in your head—and the broader organization—will be loud, screaming that you are "not enough" as a leader or that your project is doomed to fail. You will lose sight of the broader impact that you are trying to achieve, feeling more and more distanced from the meaning and purpose of your work.

It's at this point that I urge you to reach back to this book.

Remember the cloud of chaos that covered me as I was completing this book? Projects off the rails, skeptical clients, internal team issues, you name it. I was in the thick of it.

You know what I did in those difficult moments? I turned to my own book for advice. I kid you not: When I felt that I could no longer see the forest through the trees, I flipped to the chapter of the book related to the specific challenge that I was facing and read the advice that I gave myself, that I have now given you.

The great news is that, in those moments of challenge, I found the advice in these pages centering. I used the tools, just as I've described them to you, and created more unity, connection, and cohesion among the teams that I was working with at the time.

Now that this book has been released into the wild, it is my prayer that it brings the same level of inspiration and grounding to you, dear innovator—when you find yourself smack-dab in the messy middle of your own innovation free fall.

Be the Change

This isn't simply the end of this book. This is your moment—your choice point.

My question to you is this: *How will you use the knowledge that you have gained?*

Will you let this call to spread light and love in innovation go unanswered? Or will you intentionally apply what you've learned—experimenting with the challenges shared and tracking results?

Of course, I hope you'll choose the path of application. And I want to celebrate you as you do. So, please reach out to share your stories. Remember:

You're always one decision away from a totally different life.
UNKNOWN

You can't lead the people if you don't love the people.
CORNEL WEST

*Love is the deep and unwavering commitment
to the flourishing of a human.*
MARCUS BUCKINGHAM

Acknowledgments

S O MANY PEOPLE have traveled this book journey with me. I'm grateful to each one of you.

I'd like to offer special thanks and gratitude to the following people.

To my partner in life and business, Adriano Galvão, and our daughter, Livia Galvão—thank you for your endless patience and unwavering support while I wrote this book. You both made countless sacrifices as I worked through "just one more chapter." I am forever grateful for your patience.

To Emilie Jimenez, my book coach—this book simply wouldn't exist without you. You pushed when I needed it and offered grace when I needed space, and your wisdom and friendship were my guiding light throughout this journey. I'm so grateful that our paths Divinely crossed—it was no accident!

To my clients—every organization and individual served by Sylver Consulting since 2003 has influenced the pages of this book. Each project has shaped me into the innovator I am today. Thank you for trusting me and my team on your journeys. We are privileged to have had the opportunity to serve you.

To Priscilla McKinney and Will Leach—hearing about your book journeys helped me to say yes to my own. You took a dream—a calling—that felt impossible and made it feel doable. Thank you for encouraging me to embrace this project.

To my publishing team at Page Two—Jesse Finkelstein, James Harbeck, Natassja Barry, Taysia Louie, and so many more—working with you has been the joyful journey you promised. I'm so thankful our paths crossed. Special thanks to Rob Volpe, also, for stepping in and connecting me to you all when my first publisher went bankrupt and left me stranded.

To Tom Mulhern, who has, for years, been planting the seed for this book. Repeatedly, you have said, "Brianna, you have a special knack for stakeholder engagement." It took me a long time to recognize and own that gift, but now I've codified it for others—hopefully leaving the world a bit better as a result.

To Heather Dominick—your mentorship since 2015 has helped to sharpen my intuition, deepen my listening skills, and hone my visionary strengths. I now stand taller in my ability to read "between the lines," thanks to your guidance.

To my small group sisters—Grace Sakwa, Elizabeth Yamat, and Cheryl Williams—thank you for your love, support, and accountability throughout this journey. You kept me going when the going got tough, when I wanted to throw in the towel and not continue.

To Molly Fletcher—your speech at the 2024 Global Leadership Summit reignited a fire in me, showing where I'd been passive and where I needed to lean into faith to create what God had called me to do with this book. Thank you for that much-needed push. It came just in time.

To my "call a friend" resources—Corinne Brady, Peter Bürgi, Warren Corrado, Erin Duncan, Chris Grodoscki, Sabina Havalic, Paige Hendersen, Briel Kobak, Mia Lecinski, Rob Maihofer, Imran Md, Brady Nahlik, Farah Putri, Chris Rife, James Russell, Cyrus Safari, Paul Sagraves, Sheysel Sanchez, Michaela Shoemaker, Jason Taft, Jacqueline Walker, and Bob Wright—each of you, at different moments, helped recenter me, reminding me why this book was so important. Whether through thoughtful feedback or meaningful conversations, you helped me stay on track and hone key points. Thank you!

To my marketing team—Robyn Minor, Santana Wright, Enya Silveira, and Jeffrey Oelkers—your support in getting the message of this book out to the world has been invaluable. I am so grateful to have your support.

Notes

Part One: Suiting Up

p. 12   Epigraph: John C. Maxwell (@officialjohnmaxwell), "Remember this: If you're growing, you're always going to be out of your comfort zone. The more intentional you are about your growth, the greater your potential for becoming the leader you're capable of being. Never stop learning and never stop growing!" LinkedIn, June 17, 2023, linkedin.com/posts/officialjohnmaxwell_remember-this-if-youre-growing-youre-activity-7075840749761691648-PlhQ.

Chapter 3: Slay Energy Vampires

p. 39   *using the RACI model*: "RACI Matrix | Definition and Example | How to," HotPMO Ltd., hotpmo.com/management-models/raci-matrix-definition-and-example-how-to.

Chapter 4: Define Project Success

p. 55   *I call these questions the Five Intention-Setting Questions*: Heather Dominick, *Different: The Highly Sensitive Leadership Revolution* (EnergyRICH Coaching, Inc., 2022).

Chapter 5: Clarify Innovation Ambition

p. 62   *"Managing Your Innovation Portfolio"*: Bansi Nagji and Geoff Tuff, "Managing Your Innovation Portfolio," *Harvard Business Review* (May 2012), https://hbr.org/2012/05/managing-your-innovation-portfolio.

Part Two: Free Fall

p. 100 Epigraph: Pema Chödrön, *When Things Fall Apart: Heart Advice for Difficult Times* (Shambhala, 2016), 93.

Chapter 10: Watch Your Frog

p. 134   *humans have three basic needs*: Richard M. Ryan, "Psychological Needs and the Facilitation of Integrative Processes," *Journal of Personality* 63, no. 3 (1995): 397–427, https://doi.org/10.1111/j.1467-6494.1995.tb00501.x.

p. 134   *people are motivated to grow and change*: Richard M. Ryan and Christina Frederick, "On Energy, Personality, and Health: Subjective Vitality as a Dynamic Reflection of Well-Being," *Journal of Personality* 65, no. 3 (1997): 529–65, https://doi.org/10.1111/j.1467-6494.1997.tb00326.x.

p. 134   *degree to which each of these basic human needs*: Edward L. Deci and Richard M. Ryan, "Self-Determination Theory: A Macrotheory of Human Motivation, Development, and Health," *Canadian Psychology/Psychologie canadienne* 49, no. 3 (2008): 182–5, https://doi.org/10.1037/a0012801.

Chapter 11: Evolve in Real Time

p. 144   *if I may draw on the Red Ocean/Blue Ocean contrast*: W. Chan Kim and Renée A. Mauborgne, *Blue Ocean Strategy, Expanded Edition: How to Create Uncontested Market Space and Make the Competition Irrelevant* (Harvard Business Review Press, 2015).

p. 145   *LEGO® SERIOUS PLAY® methodology*: © 2025 The LEGO Group

Chapter 12: Weather the Blamestorm

p. 161   *navigate the five stages of grief*: Elisabeth Kübler-Ross, *On Death and Dying: What the Dying Have to Teach Doctors, Nurses, Clergy and Their Own Families* (Scribner, 1969).

Part Three: Safe Landing

p. 194   Epigraph: John C. Maxwell (@officialjohnmaxwell), "Leaders become great, not because of their power, but because of their ability to empower others!" LinkedIn, January 26, 2025, linkedin.com/posts/officialjohnmaxwell_leaders-become-great-not-because-of-their-activity-7289452406726172672-vzOL.

Chapter 15: Empower Implementation Partners

p. 199   *First, we conducted an ALUo Assessment*: Scott G. Isaksen, Brian Dorval, and Donald J. Treffinger, *Toolbox for Creative Problem Solving: Basic Tools and Resources* (Creative Problem Solving Group, 1998).

Chapter 16: Create and Sustain Implementation Momentum

p. 211 *delineating the team's "Rocks"*: Dean Breyley, "Managing Your Rocks," *EOS Worldwide*, eosworldwide.com/blog/managing -quarterly-rocks.

p. 212 *Step 3: Create SMART goals*: George T. Doran, "There's a S.M.A.R.T. Way to Write Management's Goals and Objectives," *Management Review* 70, no. 11 (November 1981): 35–36.

p. 215 *This challenge is a group activity*: Gino Wickman, *Traction: Get a Grip on Your Business* (BenBella Books, 2012).

p. 215 *The term "Rock" comes from*: Breyley, "Managing Your Rocks."

About the Author

BRIANNA SYLVER is the founder and president of Sylver Consulting, a globally recognized innovation research and strategy firm. Operating at the nexus of Market Research (MR), User Experience/Design (UX), and Strategy, Sylver Consulting empowers Fortune 1000 organizations and city governments to navigate change and future-proof their offerings. Under Brianna's leadership, the firm consistently uncovers actionable insights, paving clear pathways to sustainable growth and transformation.

A sought-after thought leader, Brianna is celebrated for her expertise in innovation, design thinking, user experience, and consumer insights. She has earned accolades from esteemed organizations, including the Product Development & Management Association (PDMA), HSM Management (Brazil), and the Qualitative Research Consultants Association (QRCA). Brianna is a dynamic speaker and prolific writer, frequently addressing topics such as the convergence of market research and user experience, best practices in creating and fostering innovation cultures, and reimagining civic and social systems.

Brianna's academic credentials include a BFA in communication design from the University at Buffalo and a master's degree in human-centered communication design and design strategy (MDES) from the IIT Institute of Design.

Connect with Brianna on LinkedIn at **linkedin.com/in/ briannasylver.**

What's Next?

YOU'VE TAKEN THE LEAP. You've explored the turbulence of innovation. You've confronted the discomfort that so often tempts us to pull away, to isolate, to retreat. But now you know: Transformation happens in the free fall. And the true work begins when we choose to lean in—especially when it's uncomfortable. This book is just the beginning...

I Invite You to Join the Movement

Connect with me on LinkedIn

Innovation isn't a solo sport, and I want to hear from you. How has this book shaped your thinking? How are you applying these ideas within your teams, organizations, and communities? What results have you witnessed? I'd love to hear from you! ▸ **linkedin.com/in/briannasylver**

Join the Leading Through Free Fall community

This book is an invitation to embrace love in business and to make the discomfort of change a powerful catalyst for growth, transformation, and positive impact.

Join the book's newsletter to become part of a community of leaders who are committed to transforming moments of turbulence into trust. This newsletter is your gateway to deeper conversations and insights related to the content of this book. It also opens opportunities to connect with other changemakers like yourself.

Periodically, we will bring members of the newsletter together for Community of Practice discussions, webinars, and other peer mentorship opportunities. Join the newsletter now to stay in the loop on upcoming gatherings, workshops, and new insights! ▸ **leadingthroughfreefall.com**

Share the message and spread the light
As more people embrace this way of leading, our collective impact grows stronger, creating ripples of change that extend far beyond what any one of us could achieve alone. But I need your help to spread the word. Below are a few ways you can help!

- Share your key takeaways in a review via your preferred online retailer or forum—every review helps!
- Gift the book to a friend, colleague, or leader who needs it!
- Start a book club or reading group—learning and accountability are amplified in a community. If you're interested in bulk sales, let's talk!
- Host a team workshop—let's bring these ideas to life in your organization!
- Reach out to **info@sylverconsulting.com** to arrange a workshop or bulk sales.

Success in innovation isn't about avoiding turbulence—it's about learning to navigate those moments of uncertainty, ambiguity, and resistance with courage, trust, and love. This work is bigger than any one of us, but together, we can create real change. Thank you for taking this leap with me! Now, let's keep going—spreading light, leading with love, and transforming the way in which we work and lead.